What people are saying about *Making Culture Pay*

"Visionomics' idea of corporate culture has been monumental in helping us understand our associates and how we need to relate to them—and more importantly, in teaching us how to get results."

—Gina Chatman
Owner, Kenton Brothers
Systems for Security

"Jerry Haney has an outstanding understanding of organizational culture. He continually demonstrates his ability to clearly relate his experience and knowledge to others, enabling them to become effective cultural leaders as well."

—Nancy Lauterbach
Owner, FIVE Star Speakers & Trainers

"Jerry Haney's years of experience building cultures combined with the Visionomics model gave us immediate insight into establishing a baseline for understanding our culture and, most importantly, how to work on the right components. Jerry understands how to build great cultures while maximizing a company's strategic imperatives."

—Jim Drake
Former President, Ensemble Company,
Subsidiary of Hallmark Cards

"Not only has Jerry had many years of successful experience building and rebuilding high-performance organizations, he has developed a very compelling model that will enable its followers to dramatically improve any workplace culture—at any level of the organization."

—Rich Bendis
President and CEO,
Kansas Technology
Enterprise Corporation

"I've worked with Jerry Haney for many years and found he is unparalleled in terms of his communication skills, which anchor his tremendous insight into culture development and general management. He is truly one of the 'best of the best' in his field!"

—Dave Laconi
Vice President Sales, Primary Care
Division, Aventis Pharmaceuticals

"Jerry Haney's ability to understand complex business issues combined with his knowledge of corporate cultures makes *Making Culture Pay* a must read for anyone wanting to make a bad company good or a good company great."

—Dave Duplay
Managing Director,
Life Sciences Practice,
AnswerThink Inc.

"Jerry Haney has an extraordinary ability to get frontline supervisors to understand the impact that a dysfunctional corporate culture has on their day-to-day operations!"

—Roger Crain
Senior Vice President,
Health Midwest

"Jerry has a unique understanding of how business leaders can continuously improve the performance of their organizations. Through the use of his model Jerry is able to simplify the complex subject of cultural leadership while exciting managers at every level concerning their potential for dramatically improving the results of their own workplace cultures."

—Bob Gourley
Chairman, CEO,
Lawrence Photographic Inc.

MAKING CULTURE PAY

SOLVING THE PUZZLE
of
ORGANIZATIONAL EFFECTIVENESS

JERRY HANEY

Visionomics, Inc.
Lee's Summit, Missouri

Making Culture Pay
Solving the Puzzle of Organizational Effectiveness

Copyright 2002, Jerry L. Haney

Book cover and interior design by Tim Lynch

Book publishing services by BookWorks Publishing, Marketing, Consulting

Publisher's Cataloging-in-Publication

Haney, Jerry.
      Making culture pay : solving the puzzle of
organizational effectiveness / Jerry Haney. – 1st ed.
         p. cm.
         Includes bibliographical references and index.
         LCCN: 2001012345
         ISBN: 0-9667960-0-4

1. Corporate culture. 2. Organizational change.
I. Title.

HD58.7.H36 2001   658.4'06
                QBI01-200805

Dedication

To my mother, Beatrice Haney, who demonstrated her confidence in me and in any endeavor I chose to undertake in my lifetime.

To my wife, Julia, who has given me her support and encouragement for 42 years, even when I may not have deserved them, and who has often carried more than her share of the load when the road became rough.

Acknowledgments

I have been inspired by a number of truly outstanding leaders, including those I have worked for and others I was honored to have work for me. Each has played a major role in shaping my theories on leadership and corporate culture. Therefore, each has had some part in the generation of this book.

Two icons have especially provided lasting inspiration to me and to thousands of others who were privileged to work for their organizations.

The first is Joseph C. Wilson, who had the foresight, vision and tenacity to transform a struggling photo-recording paper company into the Xerox Corporation, which subsequently developed one of the most successful products in American business, the 914. Wilson created a company that, in its heyday in the sixties and early seventies, was one of the most desirable enterprises in which to work.

The other visionary leader who remains a strong influence in both my professional and my personal life is Ewing Kauffman, founder of Marion Laboratories and the first owner of the Kansas City Royals. Starting in his basement at mid-century, Mr. K developed what became one of America's most successful pharmaceutical enterprises. Mr. K's overriding belief in common people accomplishing uncommon things led to one of the most exciting workplaces in the nation.

Leaders for whom I worked directly, and who empowered me to "do it my way," include Tom Olofson, Sid Humphreys, Harley Tennison, Brant Cotterman and David Roche.

Other great leaders for whom I didn't work personally but whose ideas and achievements have influenced my own include Fred Lyons, former president and CEO of Marion and later Marion Merrell Dow, Jim McGraw, COO of Marion, and Jerry Holder, vice president of HR at Marion.

I would be remiss if I didn't also acknowledge the long list of colleagues who have worked for me or alongside me in the more than 20 organizations I have had the honor of leading. It is my hope and belief that each one of them knows his or her role in my professional and personal development.

I want to thank Bosh Bruening and Dave Raden, my gifted partners, who have accompanied me through the thrills and challenges that come with running startup ventures. We learn every day from our experiences together.

In addition, individuals outside my business ventures have also contributed immensely to my knowledge of and opinions about leadership. They include Pastor David Frech and the "brothers" I was gifted with late in life, Bill Eveland and Jerry Simmons.

As for this book itself, it would not have been possible without the dedicated efforts of Pola Firestone of BookWorks, who served as my project manager; Kate Duffy, who was instrumental in creating the early drafts; and Paul Wenske, who did a great job of making it all come together through his editorial and writing gifts.

Finally, I wish to thank the patient friends, family and business associates who took the time to read the early drafts of this book and who gave me invaluable advice on how to make it useful to you, the reader.

All of these supporters made it possible for a person who has spent most of his working life hiring, firing, encouraging, motivating and counseling others, and whose writing prowess has been limited to creating marketing plans and proposals, to publish a book. Thanks again to each of you.

—Jerry Haney

Foreword

Jerry Haney and I began working together in the early 80s when he was a senior executive in the pharmaceutical industry and I was providing consulting support in leadership development, team building, and cultural transformation to his company as part of a recent merger. I learned very quickly that Jerry was not the usual client. He had his own ideas and models of how change occurs within an organization's culture. From the beginning he took charge of the process, rather than expecting me to provide all the expertise. We became partners, colleagues, and eventually friends because we had so much in common. We also shared a tremendous base of knowledge about culture and how to improve and change things to increase organizational performance and productivity.

I came away from our initial engagement suggesting that Jerry write a book to share his knowledge and experience with leaders in other organizations. At first, he laughed. However, as our relationship evolved, he began to take me seriously. I also suggested that if he retired from his day job, he and I could collaborate on other culture change projects and in the process have some serious fun with a variety of organizations.

Well, Jerry did both. He retired, and he wrote this book about culture and leadership and the benefits of developing a powerful corporate culture. Culture really does pay! We have also collaborated in a number of client-related activities involving culture assessment, training and development of associates and client intervention.

What is most impressive to me is that Jerry did not read a lot of other books to synthesize his own notions and theory about culture change. His lessons and insights for leaders come from his own real-world experience as a leader, which breathes a kind of "knowing" throughout these pages and the consulting services he provides to his client organizations.

—D. Joseph Fisher, Ph.D.
President, Orion International

Contents

Introduction

Whether it's put in place by plan or neglect, culture always exists. And it plays a key role in the performance and success of your organization. During my 35 years of leadership in both large and small enterprises I have found that the most intractable, hidden barrier to any enterprise's success is the lack of cultural leadership. Briefly put, companies fail to reach their true potential without the support of an effective culture.

Too often, leaders are trained primarily to be managers of processes and people. In other words, they are trained to conduct the business of working "in the house," focusing only on the assigned processes that define their workday. As a result, cultural values are unwittingly sacrificed to short-term performance goals. Few leaders are trained to step back and assess their roles within a larger context of working "on the house," examining how they go about building a high-performing culture that can quickly take advantage of the opportunities their competitors miss.

Cultural leaders work "on the house" not just "in the house"

We don't train enough leaders to understand this thing called culture, nor do we hold them accountable for helping build an organizational culture that is able not only to produce great results but also to recruit, train, motivate and retain talented people.

I wrote this book to share some of the very best ideas I've learned about organizational culture. The book will show you how nurturing your organization's culture—that invisible fabric of interwoven forces that can inspire people to embrace an enterprise with a strong sense of ownership—can complement all your operating processes and help you build a more rewarding and profitable place to work.

I want to challenge you to evaluate your present organizational culture and to set new goals and objectives to take your organization to new levels of performance, no matter how good it is today.

I also wrote this book to respond to a comment I often get from leaders: "Jerry, I can't do anything about the culture of my own department until my boss does something about the culture of the entire enterprise." One of my key goals is to erase such negative thinking and motivate you to begin improving your culture at whatever level you work. Every leader, at every level, has innumerable opportunities to dramatically improve the effectiveness of their organizational culture, regardless of what their bosses are doing.

Today, an organization's survival requires a strong and adaptive culture that thrives on change, inspires loyalty among customers and nurtures pride among associates. But great organizational cultures don't just happen. This book provides the resources to address the universal problems that plagued even the great cultures that I worked in, including Xerox Corp. during its growth years in the sixties and seventies and Marion Laboratories, which during the eighties had one of the highest rates of sales and earnings per associate of any company on the New York Stock Exchange.

Throughout my 35-year corporate career, I have held more than 20 different positions, most in sales and marketing. But I have also led organizations as diverse as engineering, quality assurance, and manufacturing, some with as few as 10 employees, others with several thousand employees. Because I was exposed to so many diverse experiences, my role evolved into one of helping new, merging or struggling divisions within larger organizations build, rebuild or improve their performance and operating culture.

My teams developed a solid reputation for turning around troubled organizations. Indeed, I created a career of moving from one organizational challenge to another, along the way becoming dubbed, with a dash of humor, "Mr. Fix-It."

I became a student of organizational culture because it was so clear to me what we as leaders often don't understand—that there are specific, definite ways to dramatically improve the culture of the organizations we are responsible for. I'm not proposing that you or I, or anyone else, can create the perfect culture. That's improbable. But I am proposing that if you can embrace six basic cultural truths, you will possess the framework for building a stronger, more productive, attractive and adaptable organizational culture than the one you have today, even if you already have a good culture. Every organization has room to improve.

Besides working inside two great organizational cultures during their greatest hours, I have also enjoyed both the exhilaration and the tears of being an entrepreneur. I have learned from my successes as well as my failures. I had one failure in a venture that had a great product idea and a great vision, but lacked the resources to commercialize its dream. That ill-fated adventure left me not only broke but also heavily in debt. Nevertheless, it was one of the best learning experiences of my life. I've worked through the anguish and become more realistic, but even more committed to finding ways to help leaders understand how nurturing their culture can take their organizations to new heights of performance and overall effectiveness.

Before you read any further, I want to emphasize that your organization must have a viable product or service to offer to its customers in order to benefit from the ideas expressed in this book. An improved organizational culture is not a substitute for the wrong product at the wrong time, or the lack of supporting resources of money, knowledge and time to build a viable business. But if you have a viable product and are looking for the best way to realize your dream of a dynamic, high-performance organization that can sustain outstanding results over long periods of time, this book can give you the framework you need to build a team that can get you there.

Our competitive business world is constantly influenced by change, and challenged by the difficult task of recruiting, motivating and retaining the very best talent. We are routinely called upon to make the appropriate adjustments to nurture and sustain outstanding performances, strong bottom-line results and enjoyable workplaces.

Look around you. Where are all the great organizations that seemed to have it made, with great products and millions of customers? The answer is that in far too many cases they've lost their edge. Their organizational cultures were unable to adapt as the world changed, as their competition changed, as the technology changed, and as the people who came to work for them changed. The same fate doesn't have to happen to you. You can begin right now to create a strong, adaptive culture that will continue to grow and prosper, and attract, motivate and retain talented workers. Let us begin the journey.

CHAPTER 1

Learning from a Rubik's Cube™: The Visionomics Model for Change

"Out of intense complexities intense simplicities emerge."

—Winston Churchill[1]

Culture is the glue that holds together all of our values, our beliefs, our sense of self, and our confidence and trust in the people around us, whether that's our family, our place of worship, our community, our nation or our company. Culture is what defines us as individuals, as citizens, as parents, as employers and as employees. Our culture is what sets us apart from other people, other organizations and other nations.

When we believe in our culture, we are motivated to protect it against all odds. In contrast, if we don't believe in our culture, we will barely lift a finger to help it survive.

We learn this early, even before we know the words to define it. Most of us learn the meaning of culture within the structure of our family. When we work together, respect each other and share a healthy core of values, the result is a caring family that will nurture our growth into caring, self-confident adults.

This carries over into school. We all have memories of how we fit into the classroom, how easy or hard it was to be accepted, and how well our teachers created environments in which we felt motivated to learn and interact with others.

My school memories are very clear. I was a hyperactive (what we would now probably call ADD) child. By the fifth grade there was a question as to who would run the class: the teacher or I. My parents and school administrators intervened, however, and I was sent to military school to learn discipline in a more structured setting. I did. You either toed the mark or you stood at attention—facing the wall for what seemed like hours.

That fifth-grade year was a turning point in my life. I learned quickly what it meant to function within a strong culture. At first, I just wanted to survive. It was plain to me that students who bought into the school's culture of results, respect and discipline got ahead. They won the special privileges, they even got their own horses assigned to them and they got promoted in rank to leadership positions. No question about it, I wanted to find a place among the successful.

I learned that a strong culture defines its core values. It might have seemed harsh at the time. There was nothing fuzzy about the demands—or the rewards. And while I never became a perfect student, I learned that I had a better chance to succeed when I knew clearly what was expected of me and operated within the boundaries of whatever culture I was a part of. I remembered those lessons and applied them diligently when I taught school for several years after graduating from college, and later when I left the teaching profession to pursue a corporate career.

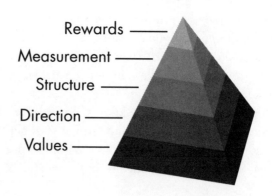

Pyramid model of cultural traits

The Visionomics Cube

During my early management positions, I was part of some great successes that often seemed like sheer serendipity. But as I analyzed these organizations, I saw that they had detectable, recurring traits. As I assumed more leadership roles, I began to see patterns that helped to explain a culture's strengths and weaknesses.

As I began to put words and definitions to these patterns, I embraced a model that resembled a pyramid made up of five basic tiers, starting with core values at the base, then direction, structure, measurement and rewards at the very top.

The model served me well for many years. But as I gained more experience with it, I began to realize that it did not completely express what I had discovered about the critical elements of culture and their interrelationships. The pyramid's form implied that the lower blocks needed to be in place before working on the ones above them but that is not always the case.

Then one night, in that lucid time between wakefulness and dreaming, the image of a Rubik's Cube™ came to mind. It dawned on me that the mechanics of solving a Rubik's Cube was a great visual metaphor for culture, as I viewed it.

The Rubik's Cube, like organizational culture, looks simple. But there are actually 43,252,003,274,489,856,000 possible ways to configure it. If you start twisting the cube, and don't know what you're doing, it merely continues to look very much like it did before you began. Hopeless.

It hit me: This is true of cultures too. You can try all kinds of management programs and processes. You can make a new strategic plan one year and create a new compensation plan the next, and follow up with management by objectives the third year. While you might see marginal improvements, in many cases, you still end up feeling like you are doing little more than twisting the cube, without really solving the puzzle of organizational effectiveness.

In fact, you'll never solve the Rubik's Cube puzzle unless you understand the 54 moves required. Solving the puzzle, like building a highly effective workplace culture, requires that each "twist" have a specific

purpose and that the move relates to the end goal of completing the cube—
or fulfilling your vision for your organization.

So, with a bow to Mr. Rubik, I created a new model to delineate the six
critical elements of organizational culture, the Visionomics Cube. At the
very center of my cube, surrounded by the six critical elements of culture,
is the stakeholder. The six elements continuously act and interact with each
other around the stakeholder to create the beliefs and assumptions each
stakeholder has about the organizational culture.

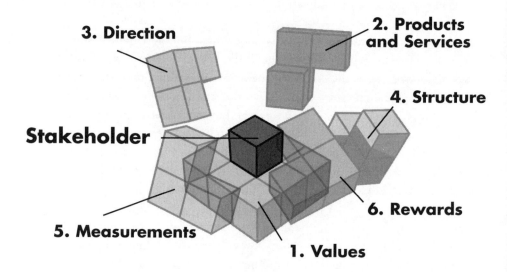

Six elements of the Visionomics Cube

The six critical elements of organizational culture are:

- *Core Values:* Our universal commitment to how we will interact
  with all the stakeholders of our organization.
- *Products and Services:* Determines who our internal and external
  customers are and forces us to assess how we are meeting their
  needs, wants and values. This information leads to understanding
  how we must continuously adapt to competitively meet those
  customer expectations.
- *Direction:* Our organization's goals, objectives and strategies that
  will allow us to achieve our purpose and vision.
- *Structure:* The element of culture that ensures that every

stakeholder is clear about who is responsible for what in the organization, and that the operating and cultural processes are as effective as possible.

- *Measurements:* The process of determining progress toward our individual and collective goals and objectives, using methods that engage employees through involvement, proper measurement and timely feedback.
- *Rewards:* The effective combination of extrinsic rewards that include economic incentives, such as salary and bonuses, and intrinsic rewards that are based primarily on non-monetary rewards.

The exercise of fitting the elements of the cube together serves as a parallel to how culture really works. For example, to reward associates effectively you need to involve them in developing their own performance measurements (measurements element). But you can't set appropriate measurements without each stakeholder having a clear sense of who is

As leaders, we ought to execute the business of the day with a mindset that we are at the same time working on the culture of the organization.

responsible for what in the organization (structure element). In addition, to move forward stakeholders need to know where your organization is headed (direction element). Furthermore, you can't develop an effective direction if you don't understand how well you meet present and future customer needs (products and services element). Of course, your core values (core values element) determine how effectively you interact with your stakeholders in carrying out the other critical elements of culture.

So clearly, there's an interdependent relationship that allows these pieces to move in harmony with each other. Understanding where your organization is in relation to each of these pieces will, in turn, help you to understand the strengths and weaknesses of your culture in terms of its potential to produce great outcomes.

Working on cultural effectiveness in no way takes away from how you approach organizational performance. Some of the cultural elements are themselves essential to organizational efficiency and effectiveness, such as setting appropriate goals, measuring performance and tying those measurements to the rewards processes.

So I'm not suggesting that you stop working on the business of the day to focus exclusively on culture. Rather, I'm suggesting that as leaders, we ought to execute the business of the day with a mindset that we are at the same time working on the culture of the organization. By working on both simultaneously we will build a stronger, more effective workplace culture and develop stronger cultural leaders for the future.

I view cultural leaders as managers who have a strong sense of their organization's purpose and also a keen understanding that they must spend a significant amount of time working "on the house," and not spend all their time working "in the house."

Taking Apart Your Cube: A New Way to Look at Culture

Building strong and adaptive organizational cultures is imperative. There's no doubt about it anymore. Whether we like it or not, we spend more time at work than we do at home. Why would you want to spend most of your life in a place you don't like? You wouldn't. Not if you can go some place else.

Many academics will tell you that great organizations are stimulated and energized by great leaders, and that is absolutely true. But I am more and more convinced that the lasting performance of an enterprise also depends critically on the performance of each of the subcultures of the organization—whether it's a branch office, a division or a department. Therefore, each subculture must become an organization that is itself an outstanding example of cultural excellence.

Let's assume you're the CEO of your company and I come to you and ask, "Are you sure John Espinoza down in manufacturing and Gail Jones over in sales and marketing have a consistent understanding of the strengths and weaknesses of your overall organization or even their own subcultures, for that matter?" The vast majority of leaders would probably respond, "I don't know what our culture is myself. So I'm sure they don't have a consistent view."

This type of response is my cue to pull out my handy Visionomics Cube and begin taking it apart. My focus is first on the stakeholder at the center of the cube, that is, every individual who is impacted by the actions of the organization—employee, customer, supplier, etc. It is those individuals' beliefs and assumptions about what is going on around them that determines how desirable that place is to be a part of. To build an organization, or any part of one, capable of reaching its true potential, we need to create an environment in which each stakeholder's four critical needs are met:

1. A clear sense of focus as to where the organization is going
2. A deep sense of personal involvement in helping the organization reach its goals
3. Reinforcement for desired behaviors and outcomes
4. Pride in the organization and the individual

As we continue our discussion, I go on to describe the six critical elements of high-performance organizations and emphasize how they interact with each other in a synergistic way to dramatically impact workplace culture. In most cases, leaders agree that the model is indeed a unique and effective way to understand the dynamics of organizational culture.

When an executive demonstrates enthusiasm concerning our discussion, I usually propose as a first step that we get together with his or her leadership team and take half a day to carefully study how the organization might benefit from using the Visionomics model.

These leadership workshops are an exciting way to begin this journey of renewal. The beginning always entails getting executive commitment. That ought to be the CEO. But it might also be the vice president of manufacturing, or the vice president of sales and marketing or any other progressive subcultural leader who wants to dramatically enhance his or her organizational culture.

For real cultural change to take place, every leader in an organization must understand that it's not going to be done by the boss alone. As leaders begin to understand the critical elements of culture and their responsibility for cultural leadership, they gain enthusiasm for their own renewal process, resulting in more momentum for cultural renewal throughout the enterprise.

An informal assessment of each organization's strengths and weaknesses is an important next step in this process. Often I encourage leaders to conduct a formal and objective assessment that will engage associates at every level in the renewal process. I recommend and use the Denison Organizational Culture Survey (which we will return to later), created by Dr. Daniel R. Denison.[2] This powerful tool, which is based on years of

---

As leaders begin to understand the critical elements of culture and their responsibility for cultural leadership, they gain enthusiasm for their own renewal process.

---

research on hundreds of organizations, can take a precise snapshot of your organizational culture and allow you to objectively compare the potential of your present culture and subcultures against other organizations.

The survey not only measures strengths and weaknesses, but also provides a way to relate the results to critical cultural traits affecting profitability, quality, sales growth, product innovation and employee satisfaction.

Armed with this new and often revealing information, we can step back and ask the key questions that make this an exciting quest: Does our organization have a clear sense of purpose? Do we have a clear and compelling vision? Are goals, strategies, tactics and objectives in place at every level and with the participation of every associate?

As a result of analyzing the critical elements of your culture, challenges can be identified and meaningful changes can be made right where the work gets done. Subcultural leaders quickly develop an understanding of the role culture plays and of their responsibility for creating healthy change.

Unlocking the Culture Within:
The Kenton Brothers Story

The matter of cultural excellence should not be viewed as a subject of only large enterprises. The following example illustrates the challenge facing smaller organizations that are revitalizing their cultures to adapt to changing markets. Kenton Brothers Inc., a premier Kansas City locksmith, had prospered handily under the dominating and patriarchal personalities who had run this gritty urban business for one hundred years.

But by the 1990s, the company's future seemed less secure, the succession of leadership was in doubt, and it was facing a new world of aggressive and technologically savvy competitors. These new rivals, a number of them started by Kenton Brothers alumni, drew from the same pool of skilled workers once controlled almost exclusively by Kenton Brothers.

The young upstart companies were expanding to fill the growing security needs of large corporations, threatening to hem in the growth of the stalwart Kenton Brothers, which catered to more traditional, and less profitable, customers. While its rivals aggressively marketed themselves, Kenton Brothers relied, as it had for years, on word of mouth, waiting for customers to find it.

Internally, the business clung to its old hierarchical style of management, in which associates had little say in day-to-day decisions, much less in the mission of the enterprise. That top-down and control-oriented structure had worked well in the past. But now, as the company faced greater competitive and technological changes, employees were increasingly less confident in its direction and as a result turnover had become a major operating issue. The venerable company seemed in danger of falling behind in the very market it once dominated.

When third-generation family member Gina Chatman joined the business, with her plans to introduce even such simple technologies as computers, voice mail and fax machines, there was an inevitable clash of old and new cultures. Gina and her mother, Stephanie Chatman, wanted to compete more aggressively and expand the business beyond keys and locks

9

to computerized security systems, serving the needs of the new high-end corporations building in Kansas City.

But Gina's desire to abruptly push the company forward only added to the turmoil.

The management conflicts spread to employees and morale sagged, to the point where something had to give. Finally, a change in the ownership and leadership of the family-run company in 1998 left Gina and her mother in charge of a troubled urban business that needed to come to grips with the direction in which it was headed. The company's confused employees didn't have a clue where the company was going, and Kenton Brothers began to hemorrhage skilled workers.

Gina asked me to help assess the culture's strengths and weaknesses. As I often do in such situations, I showed up with the Denison Organizational Culture Survey to get a snapshot of the organization's workplace culture.

The survey results were bleak. Associates didn't know the company's mission, or for that matter anything else about the direction of the organization. The survey acknowledged the lack of core values and team spirit. Worse yet, employees didn't think managers listened to them or even to the company's customers.

Clearly, the company's culture was languishing. If the company was headed anywhere, it wasn't being communicated to the associates, who had an enormous stake in the company's survival and success. Gina and Stephanie knew the company needed direction to position itself in this more competitive environment, and they were savvy enough to realize that they couldn't institute change without first working on the internal culture of the organization.

When there was no strong competition, the company made money easily. The question now was whether it would lose out to its rivals because of an inability to focus on a viable direction, consistently perform successfully and retain top employees.

It wasn't Gina's style to merely wait to see what would happen. She used the information gained from the Denison Organizational Culture Survey to size up where the company's culture was and where it needed to go. Gina and Stephanie focused not only on day-to-day operations but also on building a strong and adaptive culture.

They created departments and gave managers autonomy. They held monthly meetings to explain each new change to the associates, and let them air their opinions. For the first time, the company had declared values, a mission and an operating budget, all with input from the associates. Jobs were defined and responsibilities reinforced. Associates knew what was expected of them—and what they could expect from each other.

Instead of only locks, Kenton Brothers began specializing in electronic locking solutions for high-end alarm systems. Rather than locksmiths wearing grimy overalls, associates became professional consultants, dressed in white shirts and ties. After a period of uncertainty, when a few talented but disgruntled employees left, morale improved dramatically and the churning of employees slowed.

But a new pride isn't the only thing that has begun to blossom. So has the bottom line.

Between 1997 and the year 2006, only 14.5 million people are projected to enter the workforce, creating a critical need for healthy organizational cultures that can attract and retain talented employees.

In September of 2000, Kenton Brothers celebrated its biggest sales month in the history of the company, reporting an increase of 20 percent in sales over the previous year. Sales and profits continue to increase steadily and new records are being set almost every month.

While organizational cultures don't change with a wave of a magic wand, they will respond to appropriate moves in a surprisingly short period of time. The quest to solve the cultural puzzle is never-ending. It is a journey of great challenges, offering exciting rewards that can be measured in improved personal and organizational performance.

If You Build It, They Will Come

One of the biggest challenges facing organizations over the next few years will be the increasing shortage of talent. Between 1976 and 1986, nearly 25 million people entered the workforce. Between 1986 and 1996, about 19.5 million people entered the workforce.

The biggest tightening is yet to come. Between 1997 and the year 2006, only 14.5 million people are projected to enter the workforce, creating a critical need for healthy organizational cultures that can attract and retain talented employees.

But we're not only talking numbers. People leaving college today are demanding better benefits, salaries, stock options and bonuses. And they are less loyal, making retention one of the greatest pressures on business today.

In a phrase, it's getting harder to attract and keep high-caliber employees. Making matters worse, when an organization loses a valued associate, it can mean lost productivity as well as the added costs of finding and training a replacement.

In the pharmaceutical industry, we estimated that it cost $200,000 to find and train a new sales representative to replace one who quit. A good deal of this cost is due to lost sales while you wait for the new representative to get hired, trained and up to speed.

There's also the gamble whether the new person will fit into your culture. Some organizations are so hard pressed that they hire people with fewer skills, lowering the overall skill level of their workforce.

The result is that we begin to lower our standards, not only for whom we hire but also for what we'll let people get away with once they are hired. Thus we sabotage the potential of our organization to achieve greatness.

To avoid falling prey to these trends, I maintain that if we focus on building strong, adaptive cultures, we will attract high-quality talent. Our cultures will be such great places to work that people will do almost anything to be a part of them—and stay a part of them. The point is, if you build it, they will come.

Ask yourself, where are the truly great places to work? I'll bet you conclude there aren't that many. And since the shortage of talented workers is only going to get worse in the coming years, a strong organizational culture is now more critical than ever.

When Harley-Davidson opened a motorcycle plant in Kansas City a few years ago, it had trouble finding skilled workers who could also adapt to the plant's flattened management culture in which executives and labor leaders work side by side.

The company formed partnerships with community colleges to train hundreds of new workers, not only how to build a motorcycle, but also how to solve complex problems and read technical manuals. The costs were initially high. But the commitment paid off. Now, a job at Harley-Davidson is highly sought after.

Many organizations face another challenge: When you provide someone with new skills, that person has a better chance to leave for a higher-paying job. If you haven't built a highly effective workplace culture, you'll just keep churning workers and jeopardize efforts to maximize the potential of your enterprise or the subculture for which you are responsible. You'll find yourself becoming a training ground for workers and a source of skilled talent for your competitors. That's no way to get ahead.

Having worked in a number of high-performance cultures, I can tell you that they had a line of quality candidates waiting at the door to be interviewed. The more desirable your culture, the more dramatic your chances to attract and keep the best people.

That's my argument for a strong, adaptive culture. If you build it, they will come—and they will stay and perform.

CHAPTER 2

Is Your Organization Ready for Changing Times?

"Leadership is the attitude and motivation to examine and manage culture. Accomplishing this goal is more difficult lower down in the organization but by no means impossible in that subcultures can be managed just as can overall organizational cultures."

—Edgar H. Schein
Author, *Organizational Culture and Leadership*[3]

Today, more than at any other time, a company's long-term survival requires a strong and adaptive organizational culture that inspires the loyalty of its customers, nurtures pride within its workforce and thrives on the dynamics of change.

Success means being able to take advantage of new technologies, such as the Internet, keeping pace with expanding knowledge at the cutting edge of your industry and adroitly changing your products and services to match the shifting needs of your stakeholders.

Great organizational cultures don't just happen. When I use the term "great organizational cultures," I am referring to organizations at all levels that consistently:

- Produce outstanding bottom-line results
- Attract, motivate and retain top talent
- Successfully adapt to changing conditions

While there are no perfect cultures, those that expect to be around for the long haul have to be strong in each of those three key areas.

Consider Marion Laboratories in Kansas City. Marion was a stellar example of a culture that produced outstanding bottom-line results, and attracted and retained a constellation of great talent.

Everyone who worked at Marion during its most prosperous years felt a deep pride in his or her job and in the vision and operating principles of Marion's legendary president and founder, Ewing Kauffman.

A job at Marion set you apart in the community and in the pharmaceutical industry. You could go anywhere and hear people say of Marion, "That must be a wonderful place to work." Such praise, and envy, only reinforced every associate's pride.

Marion was a Cinderella of Wall Street in the early 1980s. It very successfully achieved shareholder wealth with its heart medicine Cardizem and ulcer medication Carafate. The drugs, originally expected to reap $200 million to $300 million per year, actually brought in more than one billion dollars per year by the late 1980s.

Its sales and marketing was a well-oiled machine fueled by energetic, disciplined and highly trained people. Marion had the highest sales and earnings per associate in the pharmaceutical industry. Hundreds of associates became millionaires. Earnings increased more than 50 percent per year for ten years in a row, creating a sense of euphoria, as if the culture was charmed.

In fact, Marion seemed to do everything right. But as blessed as Marion was, it had one very serious flaw: It lacked the crucial ability to adapt to the changing conditions in its industry, that being the ability to develop and capitalize on a strong new product pipeline. When the patent life of Marion's two blockbuster products began to run out, the company was unable to maintain its momentum. The highly successful products that enabled Marion to experience its great growth had been licensed in the early development stage and very effectively driven through the FDA approval process. Larger pharmaceutical companies witnessed the success of Marion's "search and discovery" process and began scouring the world for compounds they might license, rather than relying solely on their research and development operations. As a result, Marion faced fierce new competition for licensing these new compounds.

Marion couldn't make a timely transition from being a marketing phenomenon to becoming a creator of new, high-potential pharmaceutical products. By 1987, Marion's leaders wondered how the company could continue its success. Its main products were nearing the end of their patent protection, it didn't have any big products in the pipeline and it couldn't rely on research and development to replace the drugs that had made the company so successful in time to sustain the company's current performance.

They reluctantly concluded that the best option to safeguard Marion's assets was to sell. Marion's unique culture was soon swallowed by larger and more impersonally managed enterprises. Dow Chemical bought the company, resulting in Marion Merrell Dow; then Hoechst bought MMD, resulting in Hoechst Marion Roussel; and most recently Rhone-Poulenc Rorer bought HMR, resulting in the pharmaceutical giant now called Aventis, all in an attempt to form a competitive company with an acceptable new product pipeline.

But it was too late. Even a billboard campaign launched by successor Hoechst Marion Roussel to promote pride in its employees couldn't revive the glory. In its heyday, Marion—whose motto was "common people doing uncommon things"—never had to tell people that it was a great place to work. They knew.

The demise of Marion's great culture—it failed to successfully adapt to changing conditions—made me sensitive to the need to urge leaders at every level to focus on all three characteristics of great cultures (performance-people-appropriate change), and not just on performance for today. For the one thing you can count on today, and tomorrow, is change.

Organizational success is a continual process of renewal. Leaders at every level must be involved routinely in assessing the strengths and weaknesses of the organization, weighing them against the six critical elements of high-performance workplace cultures.

Such crucial assessments will lead to specific strategies and initiatives that guide efforts continuously, at all levels, to produce outstanding bottom-line results, attract, motivate and retain talent, and thrive on change. An essential key in this effort to build a highly effective culture, and subcultures, is knowing where to begin.

Twisting the Cube

No matter how extraordinary we think our culture is, the ultimate measure of its continued success is how well it serves the expectations of all its stakeholders. Developing the human power of the organization drives its financial capital. It is not by nurturing the bottom line that we build high-performance organizations. Rather, it is by nurturing our organizational cultures and subcultures that we build the bottom line.

To sustain success, people need to be excited by the challenge of strengthening their cultures by consistently assessing where they are today and where they want to go.

To sustain success, people need to be excited by the challenge of strengthening their cultures by consistently assessing where they are today and where they want to go. You want champions of culture, in every leadership role, committed to creating outstanding places to work.

An enterprise can't just declare what its culture is and expect its employees to embrace it. That makes culture a meaningless word. To build strong, adaptive cultures, associates have to feel viscerally motivated to be a key part of everything going on around them.

While there is no one-size-fits-all culture, you can increase the potential for people buying into the effort to develop a positive culture by communicating to them how they are integral parts of the desired changes and how they will be rewarded for their contributions and commitment.

But management often fails to communicate clearly how the changes will benefit the stakeholders as well as the organization. Because the stakeholders don't understand their roles, they often cling to the status quo—even to their complaints. The stakeholders want to know, and have a right to be told, "When we get to this better place, here's what's in it for you."

We all want stakeholders to share our vision for the future. So it can be discouraging to return from a seminar, for example, all excited about the latest trend in building quality organizations and be received by your associates with stony faces and glazed eyes.

The problem is that when you come back and talk about these new ideas that supposedly will make everyone happier and make the enterprise more productive, the associates may hear something all-together different: "Management has found a new way to make us do something we don't want to do." Why? You didn't involve their input as stakeholders in developing the proposed changes.

In many organizations today when things go wrong, someone suggests, "Let's try this or that new model"—the so-called management flavor-of-the-month approach. That's ridiculous and fatiguing.

It takes more than just twisting the cube to solve the puzzle of culture

This all-to-frequent approach simply tries to solve the puzzle of culture by twisting on the cube and hoping that all the pieces will come together, leading to dramatically improved results. But just as the puzzle isn't solved that way, culture doesn't work that way either.

The Building Blocks of a High-Performance Organization

A more effective approach to changing workplace cultures is to view the elements represented by the six outer pieces of the Visionomics Cube as the building blocks of a healthy organizational culture: core values, products and services, direction, structure, measurements and rewards.

By breaking the cube down you can study the integrity of each piece separately, and in relationship with the other pieces, with the stakeholder at the center. This approach provides elements your leaders can touch mentally, as they begin to assess where your enterprise is now and where you want it to be. By sharing this visual image, they can better identify your culture's present strengths and weaknesses: Have you laid a foundation with clear core values? Are those values understood and used by all the stakeholders?

As you work through each element of the model, you will find that you are better equipped to handle even the seemingly trivial complaints that may arise.

For example, when you look at how you measure employee performance, you might discover your associates can't perform their jobs to their own satisfaction because of frequent computer breakdowns. As you

Each team, department and division has a distinct subculture that exists as a smaller reflection of the way the associates in the enterprise at large work together, communicate, plan, solve problems, make products and provide services, form friendships, measure progress and reward success.

work through the products and services piece, you might uncover the reason why the computers are breaking down and why they're not getting fixed.

You might feel at some point that you aren't making progress with one of the pieces. You might feel like you are just twisting the cube. But by assessing that piece in relationship to the other five, you might discover you are working on that piece out of context.

For example, if you are setting meaningful measurements, you obviously need meaningful goals. By engaging employee stakeholders in setting their own goals and measurements, you allow them to share your focus on the future and their role in getting there.

So now you are involving the stakeholder in working towards the vision of where you want to take your organization.

Empowering Subcultures Boosts Cultural Renewal

No organization has just one culture. Every enterprise culture is comprised of any number of smaller individual subcultures.

Each team, department and division has a distinct subculture that exists as a smaller reflection of the way the associates in the enterprise at large work together, communicate, plan, solve problems, make products and provide services, form friendships, measure progress and reward success.

In fact, inside each subculture are usually more informal groups or cliques of employees who share common interests. These groups can become very influential in the absence of strong, positive leadership from the formal leaders of the organization. These internal influences can account for significant differences in performance between subcultures within the same enterprise. Depending on the strength of the workplace culture, the informal leaders can either positively or negatively impact the attitudes of other members of the subculture, dramatically affecting performance. As an example, one sales team may outperform all the other teams, even when those teams sell the same products at the same prices to the same types of customers.

The differences in performance can be credited in many cases to cultural leadership. Yet, too often the evolution of culture is left up to chance—or, more likely, to neglect. Managers are seldom given the knowledge to consciously build effective cultures. By training managers to become cultural leaders, you enable them to become more effective and accountable.

Indeed, to sustain a successful workplace culture it is crucial to hold every one of the leaders in the enterprise accountable for building his or her own subculture.

Each separate department and branch, of course, has different people, different personalities and different goals, but with one common purpose. So a savvy CEO will institute a model for the overarching culture that, while being sensitive to the differing personalities and functions of each subculture, provides consistency across the organization.

Defining Strong and Adaptive Workplace Cultures

Longtime organizational behavior researcher and business consultant Daniel R. Denison, Ph.D., defines workplace culture as:

"The underlying values, beliefs and principles that serve as a foundation for an organization's management system, as well as the practices and behaviors that both exemplify and reinforce those basic principles."[4]

A number of authors and researchers have studied the traits of successful businesses. In their book, *Built to Last*, James C. Collins and Jerry I. Porras describe companies with consistently strong and adaptive cultures. Called "visionary" because of their ability to sustain success over time, these companies include 3M, General Electric, Hewlett-Packard, Marriott, Merck, Motorola, Nordstrom, Procter & Gamble, and Sony.

These companies combine strong, well-defined, customer-oriented cultures with excellent products and a passion for staying current with changes in the marketplace. Their conscious decision to do what is necessary to adapt to change has consistently rewarded their balance sheets, their associates and their investors.

It's a given that many of the firms that regularly appear on the *Fortune* magazine "100 Best Companies to Work For" list perform extraordinarily well financially.

In contrast, witness the phenomenon of the dot-coms. Many of these startups were flush with cash before they even had a culture, much less a viable product. Now, their ability to adapt to a fiercely competitive Internet market is being severely tested.

Certainly, some of the dot-coms are building strong, adaptive cultures and may one day challenge Microsoft and the other high-tech gorillas that influence the Internet and computer markets. But most won't survive, because they were founded on a seemingly saleable idea, greed and ego— jumping into an undefined market to make a quick buck and then get out—without a viable business premise.

The Microsofts, Ciscos and the other companies with larger resources and established cultures will buy up many of the dot-coms that have a viable idea or product. More effective competitors will flatten others, as if hit by a speeding truck.

History suggests that a similar fate befell the railroad companies, which failed to adapt to changes in their environment and were knocked aside by the competition. Did you ever wonder why the railroads never made the transition to operate other modern modes of transportation, such as airlines?

When you study the people who ran the railroads, you find that these titans of industry restricted their focus to the railroad businesses. In their opportunistic desire for short-term profits, they failed to place themselves within the larger context of being in the transportation business. As a result, the airlines grew up around them and in short order displaced them as the main choice for long-distance passenger travel.

Though the railroad companies dominated their market, they failed to see where the future of transportation was headed, and they didn't adapt. Had their cultures been different, they could perhaps have remained dominant in the "transportation" industry.

Building Cultures That Thrive on Change

In their book, *Corporate Culture and Performance*, Harvard Business School professors John P. Kotter and James L. Heskett delineate three types of organizational cultures:

- *Strong Cultures* - These cultures are centered on the powerful leadership of an individual or small group of strong leaders.
- *Strategically Appropriate Cultures* - These cultures are just right for the times, but often falter as competition, markets and technology change.
- *Strong, Adaptive Cultures* - These cultures consistently are highly effective in producing results and are able to attract, motivate and retain top talent.

These labels and their characteristics mesh well with the six cultural elements of the Visionomics Cube. In the following I have adapted and modified them slightly to illustrate my own experience with the various culture types. For instance, I prefer to use the phrase "opportunistic cultures," rather than "strategically appropriate cultures," to illustrate my view of organizations that capitalize on the fleeting good times.

Strong Cultures Depend on Personality

Strong cultures can work well as long as they have strong leaders in place to make appropriate short- and long-term decisions. These cultures reflect the personality and inspiration of the dominant leader, and while they are often wildly successful, over time they can falter when these strong, visionary leaders leave or die without a succession plan.

The Zenith Radio Corporation is perhaps one of the best examples of this style of culture.

Zenith was a fabulous company that dominated the radio and television manufacturing industries early in the twentieth century. Commander Eugene F. McDonald, its charismatic founder, guided the enterprise for 45 years, during which time Zenith led with innovations that included the first portable radios, the first AC-powered radios and the first subscription TV system.

The enterprise might be shaped around a new technology or an innovative way of doing something better than anyone else. But if it lacks the ability to adapt to the changes brought on by the new needs of customers, new competition or faster technologies, it can end up like yesterday's news.

McDonald not only led his company to greatness, he also helped develop and was the first president of the National Association of Broadcasters.

However, as rigid as he was charismatic, McDonald made almost every major decision in the company himself. The effectiveness of Zenith was all based on McDonald's ability to make proper decisions, issuing orders and having them carried out. Everyone in the organization looked to McDonald for direction. But he left no succession plan. So after his untimely death in 1958, there was no one in the company to fill the huge void he left.

Zenith soon lost its number-one position in television manufacturing, and because of decisions that reflected the tastes and preferences of McDonald, the company had no other product lines to compete in a rapidly changing industry. Since then the company has gone through reorganizations, name changes and mergers as it struggles to survive.

Strong cultures can do well while led by their founders or other strong leaders. But over time, they do not create enviable track records. Often, managers just below the leader never gain the experience necessary to be strong leaders on their own. Or they fail to see the possibility of any movement upward and therefore leave.

Those leaders who are left behind, and who had looked to the strong leader for guidance, can suddenly feel directionless. Subcultures may even head off in different directions, weakening the entire enterprise's identity and collective purpose.

Opportunistic Cultures Are Vulnerable

Like strong cultures, opportunistic cultures work well for a period, but often falter as conditions—competition, market shifts and technology—change.

For a variety of reasons these cultures possess, in one shining window of time, the right people, the right product and the right customers. The enterprise might be shaped around a new technology or an innovative way of doing something better than anyone else. But if it lacks the ability to adapt to the changes brought on by the new needs of customers, new competition or faster technologies, it can end up like yesterday's news.

In its early days, Xerox was a strong example of an opportunistic culture because of its ability to maximize the potential of its unique technology.

In the late 1960s, Xerox as I knew it was a collection of about 80 decentralized branch offices. Despite the company's centralized approach to product innovation, the branches had a great deal of autonomy in terms of sales and marketing.

These branches (subcultures) were focused on the needs of their local customers, allowing them to react quickly to changes in the market. Loyal customers graduated from buying small copiers to larger copiers, as their needs changed. Sales teams tended to be highly motivated. They had a wide range of products and pricing plans to attract and serve more customers. There were many opportunities for advancement, recognition and reward. And the branches had autonomy to deploy resources. Thus, much of the company's early success took place in these decentralized markets that catered to local customers.

But the fortunes of Xerox changed when new managers from outside the company sought to centralize control of their products and their sales and marketing strategies. Among other things, the new central control diluted the local identities of the branch offices. Sales and marketing representatives often answered to far-off managers who, unlike the local sales teams, were unable to respond as quickly and as personally to the customers' needs.

Focusing more attention on the short-term bottom line than on the strong culture Xerox had built up, the leadership decided to place the lion's share of its marketing and sales efforts on its large copiers. This allowed the small-copier market, which had been the breeding ground for business for local branch offices, to slip away to emerging Japanese companies.

The Japanese not only became very efficient at building low-cost, high-quality small copiers, they also found that they could make large copiers. So

Organizations with a strong sense of adaptability not only demonstrate consistently outstanding performance, they also exhibit the ability to react to turmoil, adjust and speedily take advantage of opportunities their competitors miss.

soon they began to siphon away those loyal customers who once depended on Xerox to take care of their entire copier needs—from small copiers to large ones—further eating into Xerox's market share.

While Xerox still dominates the high-end of the market, the rest of the market it once presided over has largely been conceded to the Japanese. Here is another textbook case of a tremendous culture decimated because of decisions made around products and services that, in the end, failed to account for the changing needs of its customers and the market.

The leadership of Xerox was so focused on the bottom line that it robbed the energy from its once highly effective sales teams, which were the reason for the company's profitable years to begin with. The company, which has gone through a number of reorganizations in an attempt to recapture its former glory, has also failed to capitalize on the many high-potential products coming from its own research because of its continual focus on the "copier business" rather than on where the marketplace is going.

Strong, Adaptive Cultures Rule

In contrast to strong cultures and opportunistic cultures, strong, adaptive cultures remain customer-focused and learn from customer relationships. They use this knowledge and insight to make changes in their products, services and marketing strategies.

A good example of this type of culture is 3M. This company is constantly renewing itself by developing new products and effectively marketing them to both old and new customers. They have sold Post-it® notes to their Scotch Tape® customers and audio- and videotape to people who bought projection equipment.

Organizations with a strong sense of adaptability not only demonstrate consistently outstanding performance, they also exhibit the ability to react to turmoil, adjust and speedily take advantage of opportunities their competitors miss.

General Electric is an example of such a culture. This 122-year-old company grew from making light bulbs to become a worldwide conglomerate that makes space-travel components, medical diagnostic equipment, lasers and self-cleaning ovens. It operates a huge loan company, a reinsurance firm and a television network. It has filed nearly 68,000 patents and was the first corporation, outside computer companies, to invest in the Internet revolution, which it remains committed to.

Under its former chairman and CEO, John F. Welch, Jr., GE initiated a work-out process in 1988 to improve productivity, increase efficiency and reduce layers of bureaucracy that inhibited its ability to act swiftly.

Specifically, it shed any operating process that didn't make sense and sought out new business opportunities in untamed global markets. GE made "change" one of the bulwarks of its strategy for global expansion as it sought, in the words of Welch, to see the world "the way it is, not the way you wish it to be."[5] Along the way, GE was named *Fortune* magazine's most admired company.

Welch discussed his philosophy of change in a speech to his shareholders in 2000. He described GE as an organization "endlessly searching for new ideas," that was "not only comfortable with change but relished it."[6] He said an organization today that saw change as an opportunity rather than a threat "had a distinct advantage where the pace of change was always accelerating."

It is the same philosophy that Gina and Stephanie Chatman are pursuing in transforming 100-year-old Kenton Brothers from a sleepy locksmith shop that was bleeding workers into a powerful electronic securities firm. To open itself to new ideas, the company has broken down walls between management and associates, flattened bureaucracy and nurtured an environment where people have a say in the direction and vision of the organization.

"I believe in hiring people who are better than I am at certain things, and then allow them to flourish," says Gina. "We wanted a place where people were knocking the doors down to be a part of us."[7]

As the workplace shifts from manufacturing to managing information, placing more emphasis on cognitive abilities, organizations will require cultures that take even greater advantage of the shared knowledge of their workforce to benefit from change.

Associates increasingly will have multiple responsibilities that require cross-training to keep up with the demands of changes in the increasingly global economy.

Strong, adaptive cultures do not just happen. They are built block by block by leaders who understand the need to develop cultures where people are proud to work and that broadcast their values to their customers.

Leaders who develop the strength, speed and adaptability of their cultures will not only increase their ability and mandate to lead but spur a work culture ethic that results in greater sustaining productivity and high performance.

Testing Your Cultural Conscience

At the end of this and each of the following chapters is a checklist of questions to help you judge the present cultural potential of your organization.

If you answer yes to all the questions, feel assured that you currently have or are well on your way to building a high-performance workplace culture. If you answer no to any question, you may want to focus on that related issue as a priority as you begin your cultural renewal process.

(Answer for the culture or subculture that you are responsible for)

Cultural Conscience Checklist	Yes	No
• Is your organization performing as well as it can in terms of bottom-line results?		
• Are you happy with your organization's ability to attract, motivate and retain top talent?		
• Is employee turnover hurting productivity and/or performance in your organization?		
• Is your organization able to quickly anticipate the need for change? Does it readily make the changes required?		
• Do the leaders in your organization have a good understanding of organizational culture and how to improve it?		

CHAPTER 3

Core Values: The Foundation of the Organization

"Genuine success does not come from proclaiming our values, but from consistently putting them into daily action."

—Kenneth H. Blanchard & Michael O'Connor
Authors, *Managing by Values* [8]

Core Values Element Defined:

The four to six words or statements that make up the core values reflect the basic principles that guide our interactions with every stakeholder of the organization. They also establish the boundaries of behavior for all associates of the culture or subculture.

The Process:

■ Determination of core values
■ Effective communication
■ Reinforcement
■ Enforcement

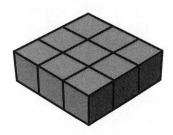

Highly effective organizations share a common quality that sustains their success and sets them apart as great places to work: a strong set of deeply imbedded and broadly held core values. They may be few in number but they are powerful in defining the manner in which associates are expected to interact with and treat other stakeholders both inside and outside the organization.

Core values establish the foundation of the culture. Until we decide what those values are, and how we will interact with each other, it's very difficult to do anything else—whether setting goals, establishing measurements, solving problems or even making decisions—effectively. As such, core values cannot be left to chance and allowed to emerge through unconscious neglect.

> *Core values establish the foundation of the culture. Until we decide what those values are, and how we will interact with each other, it's very difficult to do anything else effectively.*

Core values determine whether people work in an open and trusting environment where opinions are valued, or in an environment that is tainted by suspicion and tension. Our societal values respect open communication. The principal reasons are that open discussion tempers truth, builds trust and fosters wiser decisions. Why should we expect anything less from our work environments? Few would say they thrive in an environment where they are criticized for sharing how they feel or are worried whether their personal values are in conflict with those of the people with whom they work. In environments like that, associates walk around as if on eggshells, afraid to say anything.

Positive core values allow us to identify with an organization. They tell us where we stand in relation to the goals of the organization and empower us to ensure the credibility of our organization in the eyes of customers. Values, espoused or not, exist in every organization. Often they are historical in nature, based on what has worked in the past. Too often, the espoused values we desire for our organization are not effectively communicated, reinforced or enforced. As a result, they become forgotten, ignored or replaced by the values of individual managers or other associates, creating a confusing hodgepodge and leading to less than stellar performance.

Values can vary from one organization to another, even among those in the same enterprise. Individual departments and divisions may even have their own core values. Even so, they have to consistently reflect the core values of the overarching or enterprise culture.

Effective core values also provide clear expectations of personal interaction and set boundaries beyond which behavior becomes objectionable. For example, if a core value is integrity in everything we do, every member of the culture is expected to honorably fulfill all of his or her obligations and commitments to stakeholders of the organization. If another core value is treating every stakeholder with dignity and respect, one might vehemently disagree with an associate's opinions or actions but is expected to deal with the issue at hand without personally attacking the associate personally.

Without these institutionalized values an organization lacks the ability to reach its full potential in developing its human capital, necessary for optimizing long-term success. Indeed, without consistent application of the organization's core values, stakeholders do not know what to expect from one day to the next, and so are often emotionally, spiritually and mentally unavailable to assist the organization in reacting and adapting to changing conditions.

Role of Leadership

Our role as cultural leaders is to build an organization that encourages associates to become more focused, involved and committed to outstanding individual and collective performance. That responsibility envisions leading as many associates as possible into an inner circle of involvement for the purpose of creating a feeling of being part of an elite organization.

Typically, a leader has three main categories of associates in his or her organization, differentiated by their relationship to this inner circle. The closer they are to the inner circle, the more committed, effective and happy they are. The three categories include:

Desirable associates: These seemingly self-motivated employees are always there for you, consistently performing at high levels. They are the model of what you want every employee to be like.

Acceptable associates: These employees are less than ideal but perform at an acceptable level that enables you to consider them as ongoing participants in the organization.

Unacceptable associates: These employees never perform up to their own potential or to the organization's standards. They seem more like liabilities than assets.

Our role as cultural leaders is to create an organizational culture that encourages every associate to move into the center circle of high involvement by developing a workplace culture that gives every associate a sense of belonging and being an integral part of the organization's success. Unfortunately, there may be a few associates who can't or won't make the move into the acceptable or desirable category. There comes a time therefore when the leader must deal with these employees, even if it means moving them out of the organization.

When associates feel they are part of an inner circle, they become more confident of their leaders and more excited about their own potential and the potential of the organization. Its purpose, vision, goals and objectives become their own, and they commit themselves to helping move the organization to a better place. The cultural renewal process helps leaders identify associates who will move toward the inner circle, and those who will not. Obviously, the more associates who move to the inner circle, the easier it becomes to move the enterprise forward.

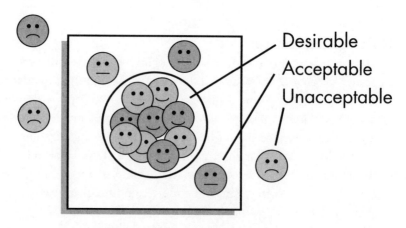

The relationship between categories of associates
and the inner circle of involvement

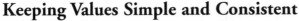

Keeping Values Simple and Consistent

You don't need long lists of core values. In fact, simplicity is preferred, as it allows associates to more easily internalize, communicate and remember the values.

When Rockville, Maryland-based Manugistics, Inc., found itself buffeted by the turbulent software industry in the 1980s, the company drafted a set of three simple core values that emphasized collaboration with clients and flexibility.

1. We treat others as we would like to be treated.
2. Partnership with our clients results in superior products.
3. Team success is more important than personal glory.

In the April 1997 edition of *Workforce* magazine, CEO William Gibson of Manugistics was quoted as saying "that success depended on a company's values being tied to its business strategy." [9]

He was proved right. Management, employees and clients brainstormed together to create three "Elements of Excellence" shortly after the company was purchased from Fortune 500 company Contel Corp. Gibson said defining the organization's core values helped Manugistics steer through a domestic and global acquisition, sale of a product line, growth of its workforce, a public offering and departure of two of its founders.

Like other visionary companies, Manugistics has used its core values to help attract and retain talented staff. Turnover is low, and employees understand that the company's incentive and reward system is tied to its core values system. Training and education are important; for example, each employee has his or her own individualized curriculum in Manugistics University, the company's year-round training and development program.

As the *Workforce* magazine writer pointed out, Manugistics understood that employees who feel empowered are as much "a selling point to potential clients" as the company's multimillion-dollar products and services. Developing its human capital, company leaders said, contributed to the bottom line. The company's stock rose from $7 a share in 1994 to more than $48 in 1996, by the time it had become a worldwide company.

Values Help Define an Organization

Because the essential goal of having values in the first place is to help us clearly understand what is expected of us, values help define the structure in which we work together. Core values accomplish this by:

- Delineating the principles for interactions between all stakeholders
- Communicating those values in a consistent and forceful manner
- Building a basis for reinforcement and enforcement of organizational values
- Providing a basis for personal and organizational accountability
- Setting the boundaries for acceptable behavior for all associates

The simple four to six words or statements that are used to express an organization's core values shape the interactions between the organization and its stakeholders—associates, customers, suppliers and community members. How stakeholders are treated dramatically affects whether they want to be associated with the organization. And this ultimately affects how the organization and its associates are perceived by outside observers. We have little or no control over how our employees treat customers if we don't build a clear system of principles to guide their interactions.

During its heyday, before it was bought by larger and more impersonal organizations, Marion Laboratories had consciously developed a culture second to none. People lined up for the opportunity to work there. Even before its highly profitable years during the 1980s, Marion developed a complete system of values and a complement of associate responsibilities that set a standard for relationships and communication.

Not only did Marion's core values help steer the company through difficult periods of growth, they came to epitomize the company's success, as the values were quoted as much as the company's stock price. As reflected in the following reprint of Marion's values statement, these values included being treated as an individual, having a safe workplace and support for personal and career growth. In return, associates were expected to make the company successful through high productivity and a commitment to excellence.

Foundations for an Uncommon Company

Our Relationships:

*W*e should treat others as we would be treated ... with dignity and respect, integrity and honesty. This applies to:

* Associates & their families
* Customers
  Consumers
  Health Care Providers
  Wholesalers
* Stockholders
* Suppliers
* Financial Community & General Public.

Those who produce should share in the results. Each Marion associate has the right to:

* Be treated as an individual
* Be rewarded for performance
* Know what is expected on the job and where we stand in relation to that expectation
* Get problems resolved and be heard
* A safe and healthy workplace
* Share in the growth of the company through personal & career growth. We earn these through our high productivity and commitment to quality in all that we do.

Our Responsibilities:

1. We have a responsibility to our shareholders to build the business on their behalf. This requires prudent investment in the development of the people, products, and facilities necessary to sustain long-term growth in profits and return on shareholder investment.

2. We have a special responsibility to our associates, our customers, and to society to provide products and service of the highest quality and to conduct our business with integrity and the highest ethical standards.

3. Risk taking is an inherent factor in business, and we are prepared to manage high risk relative to our markets—but any risk should be taken by the corporation itself and never at the expense of the consumer, the customer, or any Marion associate.

4. We have a responsibility for excellence and innovation ... We do all that we do to the very best of our ability and with the strongest enthusiasm we can generate. It is the very nature of our business to do things that have never been done before and for which there are always reasons they cannot be done. Success for us requires the ability and the spirit to find a pathway through any obstacle, even when no pathway is visible at the start.

Highlights of the above statements are emphasized on the following pages.

Valuing Our Relationships

- Treat others as we would like to be treated: with dignity, respect, integrity, and honesty.

This value came directly from Marion's legendary founder, the late Ewing Kauffman, who believed in being fair to people and to other companies. Kauffman would honor a relationship with a longtime supplier rather than buy cheaper raw materials from someone he didn't know. Treating others with dignity and respect meant that even though you might take exception with someone, you still treated the person as a valuable human being.

- Those who produce should share in the results.

This value exemplified a powerful effort to let everybody in the organization benefit by individual and collective success. If Marion reached its goals, whether you were a salesperson or a secretary, you received a bonus. But that bonus was bestowed upon you based upon your own individual performance as well. So individuals and organizations were measured regularly, and those who produced the greatest results got the greatest percentage of the payout. But the values also created boundaries. It said that if you didn't produce, you wouldn't share in the rewards. Consequently, associates knew clearly what was expected of them and where they stood in relation to that expectation.

Our Responsibilities

The company's associate responsibilities underscored how seriously associates took their commitment to the organization's ultimate success:

- We have a responsibility to our shareholders to build the business on their behalf. This requires prudent investment in the development of the people, products, and facilities necessary to sustain long-term profit growth and return on shareholder investment.

- We have a special responsibility to our associates, our customers, and to society to provide products and services of the highest quality and to conduct our business with integrity and the highest ethical standards.
- We realize risk taking is an inherent factor in business. We are prepared to manage high risks related to our markets. Nevertheless, any risk should be taken by the corporation itself and never at the expense of the consumer, the customer, or any Marion associate.
- We have a responsibility for excellence and innovation. We do all that we do to the very best of our ability and with the strongest enthusiasm we can generate. It is the very nature of our business to do things that have never been done before.

Every organization has values, whether purposefully selected or allowed to develop through unintended neglect.

Values Set the Standard

Every organization has values, whether purposefully selected or allowed to develop through unintended neglect. For example, if it is acceptable to talk about people behind their backs, then that becomes an operating norm. If, on the other hand, one of your core values is "open and honest communication," leaders and associates who hold themselves responsible for consistently following the organization's core values won't tolerate malicious gossip.

Surveys consistently show that many managers don't recognize the importance of values. Some executives believe their employees, customers and investors do not understand the company's values and goals. Likewise, employees often think their managers fail to live up to their stated values.

When I work with a company, I usually find that while most employees are aware of some kind of company values statement, only a small number say they believe management actually models and enforces those values. In other words, management doesn't walk the talk.

I was told of a particularly disturbing incident recently while working with a company. A supervisor began reprimanding an employee in public for failing to move a vehicle quickly enough to suit the supervisor. But because the scene was played out in front of his colleagues, the belittled employee began to yell back, and the situation grew into a huge debacle.

It was a nightmare for the employee, a nightmare for the supervisor, and ultimately a nightmare for the organization because of the questions raised in the minds of shocked onlookers about how the business was run. If this organization truly enforced a core value that said "we treat every stakeholder with dignity and respect, regardless of the situation," this embarrassing scene would never have taken place.

Treating other stakeholders with respect also applies to arbitration between an organization and its union.

In the absence of core values, what does your organization have as a basis for determining how people will interact with each other? How does the organization set and enforce boundaries of behavior?

Having clear core values can also provide much-needed insight when you are questioning job applicants and trying to determine whether they are a good fit for your organization. It is a simple matter to determine if applicants' values match those of the company by presenting them with a dilemma in which their core values are tested.

In most cases, having clear core values is an attraction to good applicants. People are naturally excited about the prospect of becoming involved in an organization that nurtures and supports their core values. So core values become a selling point. You want an organization brimming with associates who identify with the kind of people who are already oriented to your value system. I find it revealing that many highly successful and profitable companies, including those listed below, place service ahead of profits in their core values.

- **Procter & Gamble** - *Product excellence, continuous self-improvement, honesty, respect and concern for the individual.*
- **Wal-Mart** - *To provide value to customers, to buck conventional wisdom, to work with passion and commitment, to run lean and to pursue even higher goals.*
- **Marriott Corporation** - *To give friendly service to guests, provide good food at a fair price and work hard to make a profit to create more jobs.*

Clearly, to the degree you are able to develop, communicate and institutionalize core values, they will either play a big role in how you nurture the success of your organization or they will play no role. But without them, it is impossible to maximize the human potential of any culture or subculture.

Institutionalizing Core Values

Despite their almost universal presence, high-sounding words or phrases written on a plaque in the lobby of a home office are often no more than concepts strung together in response to just one more model program or conjured up in a burst of energy disconnected from any genuine effort to internalize them.

Only when those inspiring words or phrases become an integral part of the very fabric of the organization—when associates are holding themselves and all those around them accountable for actually living those words—do they truly represent the core values of the organization. Institutionalizing core values is much more difficult and time-consuming than simply selecting or determining what the values will be.

So how is the process of "institutionalizing core values" accomplished? The process involves five steps: determining, validating, communicating, reinforcing and enforcing the core values.

Determining the Core Values

When the Kansas City Area Transportation Authority (KCATA) asked me to help rehabilitate its flagging organizational culture, we set about developing a set of core values from scratch.

First we formed a task force of about 20 associates, who represented a diverse group of bus operators, mechanics, maintenance workers, union representatives and directors of KCATA's 750 employees. The group was given authority to select the initial core values for the organization, whose employees were expected to understand these values and live by them.

I always begin this exercise by distributing a list of 50-plus value-based words, along with definitions, using a process developed by fellow organizational consultant Joe Fisher, a friend and founder of Orion International.[10] Examples of these value-based words include:

- *Dependability* - To be counted on; to be trusted; to be relied on.
- *Integrity* - To act according to one's word; to behave consistent with one's values; to "walk the talk."
- *Profitability* - To be economically vital and viable; to produce a gain from one's investments; to have excess of capital; to use one's resources well.

After an interactive discussion concerning the objectives and methodologies of the exercise, the process commences as follows:

Step One: Each associate chooses two values (from the list of 50 suggested words and their definitions) he or she feels are most important to the organization's culture. (10 to 15 minutes)

Step Two: Associates pair up and "negotiate" their four combined value words down to three. (10 to 20 minutes)

Step Three: The pairs of associates combine to form groups of four, who negotiate to reduce their separate sets of three value words per team down to four for the combined group. (15 to 20 minutes)

Step Four: The four-member groups combine into groups of eight to ten and reduce their separate sets of words into a list of five proposed core values. Group representatives are chosen from these teams to report the selections to the task force. (20 to 30 minutes)

Step Five: Representatives from the two remaining groups present their five values and explain why their groups feel their choices are the most critical to improving the organization. At the end of the presentations, the resulting list will include five to ten different words vying for adoption. (20 to 30 minutes)

Step Six: In the final step, each member of the task force is asked to vote for the three most important values, with the purpose of winnowing down the number of value words to no more than six, which are then presented to the executive leadership for final validation.

After going through this revealing process, the Kansas City Area Transportation Authority chose the following values:

- Service to our stakeholders
- Respect for the individual
- Integrity in all that we do
- Employee involvement
- Quality in all we do
- Innovation in meeting stakeholder needs

Validating the Core Values

The next step in finalizing the recommended core values is to gain concurrence from top management. Because it comes from a broad representation of the organization, the list of core values carries a lot of validity. A savvy executive leadership realizes the opportunity for widespread acceptance. So, while normally some valuable discussion takes place, there is seldom any serious challenge to the chosen values.

In adopting the core values, the leadership is validating the choices. The true commitment to the chosen values now depends on communicating, reinforcing and enforcing those values so that they become institutionalized into the fiber of the organization.

Communicating the Core Values

Communicating the core values of an organization is an effort that, unless it becomes routine, can lose its energy over time. Both leaders and associates must make an effort to communicate the values daily. In addition, a "kick-start" promotion with fanfare is an effective way to begin to institutionalize your core values.

There are many ways to creatively communicate core values. Colorful signs, presentations and skits all can be used to make a lasting impression. Coffee mugs, paperweights and computer screen savers are also imaginative aids to help provide constant reminders of the organization's core values.

Many organizations dedicate a portion of each employee newsletter to values and share examples of people carrying out those values in executing their workplace responsibilities.

Any of these ideas can be an effective kickoff to formalize the adoption of new core values. Of more importance, though, is the leaders' enthusiasm and commitment during this critical period, and from this point forward.

Reinforcing the Core Values

No matter how effective the initial communications, the most critical factor is how organizational leaders go about "living the values."

Employees will be watching carefully to see if the leaders are serious about the values themselves. It is key that as they become cultural leaders, managers hold themselves and each other accountable to the core values.

Some suggestions that have been successful in reinforcing values include integrating them into recruiting materials and orientation; underscoring their importance with a "Value of the Month" or "Value Employee of the Month" award; and including in each newsletter an article or column featuring one value and how associates live that value at work.

On a recent visit to the Mutual of Omaha offices I noticed the leadership selected a Value Employee of the Month given for an associate's consistently positive behavior or for carrying out an act that exemplifies one of the company's values.

Enforcing the Core Values

Unfortunately, no matter how hard you work, some employees won't take core values seriously. If leaders don't hold everyone accountable for abiding by these carefully selected values, they soon become empty aphorisms. By continuing to tolerate the actions of employees who ignore the organization's values, you allow their actions to become the organization's values, which defeats the purpose of having core values in the first place.

I have witnessed this scenario often in my 35 years of organizational leadership. Team members bring to the leadership's attention an associate who seems unwilling or incapable of living up to the organization's core values. The confounding factor is that the individual involved is sometimes an outstanding individual contributor. For that reason, leaders are sometimes reluctant to deal aggressively with the situation.

But inaction reflects negatively on the leadership's commitment to the values. If the leaders do not enforce the values, their associates won't take them seriously. When one employee is allowed to ignore the organization's values, it immediately lowers the degree of importance that is placed on those values. I don't believe any one individual is worth that.

Coaching and counseling will work with many who test the leadership's commitment to the core values in the beginning, but sometimes there is that one individual who simply refuses to accept the organization's values. The fact is, when people who constantly act in a way that shows they don't share the values of their colleagues are firmly dealt with, the other associates most often quietly, or even openly, cheer.

> *When one employee is allowed to ignore the organization's values, it immediately lowers the degree of importance that is placed on those values.*

When an organization's core values are in place and have become the behavioral norm, the associates will accept, continuously demonstrate and protect the core values as "the way we do things around here."

It starts at the top. To truly institutionalize the espoused values so that they become the operating norm, the CEO and every other leader must embrace, reinforce and enforce the values on a daily basis. It can't be said enough—we demonstrate our commitment or lack of commitment to our core values by how we act as leaders.

Cultural Conscience Checklist	Yes	No
• Does your organization currently possess a set of four to six core values?		
• Are the core values communicated continually throughout the organization?		
• Are the values discussed with new employees during orientation?		
• Do leaders in your organization "walk the talk" concerning the organization's espoused values?		
• Do associates consistently live up to the core values?		
• Are the core values reinforced and enforced throughout the organization?		

CHAPTER 4

Products and Services: The Continuous Link to Customers

"In an increasingly competitive environment, providing top value for a price is a rapidly moving target. To sustain growth, a firm has to refine current products continually as well as introduce new ones faster than its competitors."

—Christopher Meyer
Author, *Fast Cycle Time* [11]

Products and Services Element Defined:

Provides a process for ensuring that every stakeholder in the organization clearly understands who our customers are and how our products and services are meeting their needs, wants and values today, and what we must do to ensure that we continue to meet those needs in the future.

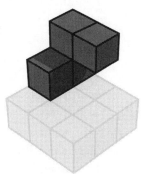

The Process:

- Clarify who our customers are today and who they will be in the future
- Determine our ability to meet present and future customer needs
- Anticipate required changes to products and services
- Initiate the required changes

Study the headlines in the business section of any newspaper and you're sure to read horror stories about organizations coming apart at the seams: bankruptcies, buyouts, layoffs, cutbacks and attempted reorganizations.

You're likely to read how the organizations were seemingly blind-sided by changes in their industries, or by competition or technology shifts. In some cases they couldn't hold on to quality employees or differentiate their products and services from those of their competitors.

What you may not read is how these organizations' cultures contributed to their inability to sustain themselves. That's because, despite much being written about culture in the last two decades, only a relatively few enlightened organizations are making their cultures pay. Culture is not

Successful leaders know that nourishing a strong, adaptive culture pays off in the way their organizations deliver on the distinctive products and services they produce.

some nebulous, New Age, feel-good concept. Successful leaders know that nourishing a strong, adaptive culture pays off in the way their organizations deliver on the distinctive products and services they produce.

Read between the lines and you'll sometimes find that the real issues weren't around the products or the strategy of the organization but that the enterprise couldn't compete because of ineffective operating parts or subcultures. If an organization can't depend on one or more of its critical components, such as research, development, manufacturing, marketing and sales or distribution, it can quickly fall behind in its ability to compete in the marketplace. So if the enterprise as a whole is to reach its full potential, it is critical that every part and level of any enterprise has highly effective workplace cultures.

Size and experience do not make organizations immune from cultural apathy. Even venerable companies such as General Motors, Texas Instruments and Colgate have failed to adapt their products and services to changes in customer preference or remained stratified and stultified in their management while their rivals attracted and celebrated innovative employees who pushed their organizations ahead at warp speed.

To build stamina and stay ahead of the competition in today's fast-paced business climate, an organization—and each of its integral parts—must be able to quickly change strategies, adjust product lines or services and find new markets while continuously striving to be as effective as possible at every level. Strong, adaptive cultures thrive on change. They possess a nimbleness of foot that traditional organizational cultures often lack.

Strong, adaptive cultures can rapidly modify or redirect their products and services to keep pace with the needs and expectations of their external customers, those who use their products and services, while nurturing the needs and expectations of their internal customers, the associates in the organization's departments, branches and subdivisions, who work in concert to produce and market those goods and services. Addressing the needs, wants and values of both these customer groups is critical.

A discussion of the role products and services play in organizational culture naturally follows the discussion of core values. For beyond reflecting the organization's desire and ability to make money, products and services also symbolize in a unique way the organization's overarching belief system. A test of your unwavering commitment to making your culture pay is whether the values and behaviors you set in place to guide the daily activities of your associates result in products and services that differentiate your organization from your competitors.

Producing and selling a better product will set your organization apart from the rest of the pack, at least temporarily. But as we've seen, to sustain that success, to enrich the strategies that propel an organization ahead and keep it there, requires a strong, adaptive culture.

In a positive culture that reflects openness, trust and pride, associates throughout the organization embrace a shared desire for success. And if the culture encourages ownership and accountability, associates will take personal responsibility for developing and delivering the organization's products and services in new and innovative ways to both their external and internal customers.

Attracting associates who share the organization's core values strengthens its culture. Examples of such distinctive cultures include Southwest Airlines, whose associates—from baggage handlers to gate attendants to pilots—place a high value on getting passengers to their destinations on time and with the fewest headaches possible; 3M, whose associates share the organization's preoccupation with producing innovative products; and Microsoft, whose associates support a near fanaticism to bring new products to the market that influence and marshal the direction of the computer industry.

Addressing the products and services piece of the culture puzzle opens the door for dramatic results. The organization improves its ability to meet or exceed internal or external customer needs and expectations. Associates feel more secure—clear in their understanding of their own roles, the goals and mission of the organization and how the organization's products and services stack up against the competition.

Selling an Experience

A good example of a business making culture pay in a highly competitive industry is Amy's Ice Creams, a super-premium ice cream business with seven retail shops in Austin and Houston, Texas. While most people might dismiss ice cream shops as more or less identical, Amy Miller had other ideas.

To differentiate her ice cream shops from all the other shops that scoop and dip their ice cream in pretty much the same way, Miller chooses to sprinkle her servings with loads of entertainment, in effect selling an experience with every banana split. On any Friday night you might see employees juggling their serving spoons, tossing scoops of ice cream to one another, break-dancing on the freezers or reciting whimsy and handing out free samples while dressed in pajamas, Star Wars masks or any other outlandish garb that spells fun to customers.

Now, fun is a good strategy by itself. But, as described by a writer for *Inc.* magazine, the real source of Miller's competitive advantage isn't just the strategy, "it's how she makes the strategy work. The real secret to her company's success is its corporate culture."[12]

Miller's way to make sure her customers always have the same, fun-filled experience that sets her stores apart "was to create and nurture a culture that made that experience inevitable. She had to get the right people and get them to behave in the right way. And because their behavior needed to be inventive and unflagging and self-initiated, she somehow had to get them to know what the right way was, without being told."[13]

For Miller, communicating the values of an innovative and inventive culture to her associates begins the moment they interview for a job. Applicants are given a plain white paper bag and asked to fashion it into some creative new form. Someone who doesn't feel comfortable turning a bag into a puppet, a game, a palate for cartoons or a rare headdress isn't going to be right for an Amy's Ice Creams shop. But associates who value humor and fun in the workplace are a good fit at Amy's.

And the bottom line reflects their success at what they do. For such energetic high jinks keep customers coming back for more premium ice cream. Customers also remember their pleasurable experience when they

Once you have an acceptable level of product quality and consistency, the best way to increase the effectiveness of your selling effort is to focus on the way you deliver the product.

choose to pull a carton of Amy's Ice Creams from a grocery store freezer that also features Ben and Jerry's, Edy's, Breyers and other national brands. Happy customers are the reason why Amy's Ice Creams is growing about 20 percent a year in a niche many would consider to be saturated.

When an organization's culture lives its values and gives its associates a feeling of ownership in turning those values into success, the whole enterprise is invigorated with a sense of power, allowing it to adapt and grow.

Consider again Kenton Brothers. When the new management sought to expand from being a simple locksmith firm to one that catered to the more complex security demands of large corporations, it empowered its associates to help the organization succeed.

Trading their grimy overalls for professional-looking suits and ties, the former lock technicians were trained to become consultants, versed in assisting clients in building large computerized security systems that met both current and future needs. The new management replaced the former top-down culture, which discouraged initiative, with a more inclusive one that encouraged greater autonomy to make decisions, and rewarded associates for making decisions that pumped up sales. By nurturing personal growth, the organization created a flexible culture able to adapt quickly to and profit from changes in its growing industry.

In other words, once you have an acceptable level of product quality and consistency, the best way to increase the effectiveness of your selling effort is to focus on the way you deliver the product—putting the sizzle in the steak, as the saying goes. How well your sales team relates to your customers, how hard and how smart your sales staff works, and how well your sales department relates to your marketing department, is reflected in customers wanting to buy your products. Amy's recognized that you can create a differential advantage with customers by making the delivery of ice cream entertainment.

The same is true of Southwest Airlines, which doesn't hire people who aren't capable of having fun at work or who don't naturally enjoy helping people. That is reflected in the services Southwest associates provide, their willingness to go to great lengths to please their customers, even singing or celebrating a passenger's birthday, or, at the very least, expressing empathy for a customer with a problem. Is it any wonder Southwest is growing in a competitive market in which many other airlines are struggling?

Of course, these are not services offered in a vacuum. They are cultural strategies that are integrated with the organization's direction, its purpose and vision for the future, its measurements and reward systems, and its overriding purpose to build sales and make a profit.

Internal Customers

When we talk about products and services, we must be clear that we aren't simply talking about our ultimate external or consuming customers. We are talking about the output of any and all of the departments, subdivisions and branches within the enterprise. The accounting department, for instance, may not produce a product for external consumption but it provides crucial services that help finance the manufacture of a product. In the same way, the marketing department services the needs of its customers in the sales department, while the research department provides its services to stakeholders in the marketing and sales departments.

Upstream/Downstream

The relationships between internal and external customers might be portrayed as if you were looking upstream and downstream from the point of view of the marketing department:

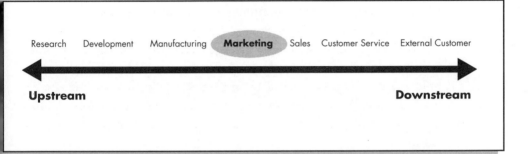

The marketing department has customers both upstream and downstream. As an example, upstream are research, development and manufacturing divisions. Downstream are sales, customer service and the ultimate external customer who consumes the enterprise's products. Viewed this way, it is easier to see that every stakeholder has a relationship with the development, production and delivery of any product.

A marketing department nurtures trust by building a strong relationship with the sales department downstream, as well as with the research, development and manufacturing departments upstream. In contrast, if the marketing department ignores the needs, wants and values of the sales department, the two divisions end up at odds with one another. It is crucial, therefore, for a marketing team to build a relationship with its sales team that is as positive as the relationship with its external customers.

The benefit of this view is that you are conscious of your stakeholders' needs, wants and values both upstream and downstream as you bring new products to market.

You may develop products in response to the needs, wants and values of your ultimate customers downstream. On the other hand, research may develop a whiz-bang idea, like the sticky note, in which case manufacturing and marketing serve the needs of research in creating effective ways to market the product.

So when you pause to analyze who your real customers are, you are really addressing stakeholders both outside and inside the enterprise. When we talk about the enterprise as a whole, we are talking about culture—the shared beliefs and values of every department and each associate.

The approach is just as useful for organizations that provide a service as it is for those that manufacture products. Consider the bus company. It's easy to mistakenly think that the most important stakeholders in the bus company are the drivers, because they are closest to the ultimate customer, the passenger. But when you look upstream, you see that if the buses are broken down, they are unavailable for service. So vehicle maintenance is just as important in the bus company. Yet, maintenance teams can't do their jobs if they can't get the necessary parts to repair or maintain the engines, and so on.

The point is that everyone, whether upstream or downstream, is, or should be, critical to the success of the enterprise. Leaders of organizational subcultures who understand this truth and take the time to nurture relationships with their internal customers will, in the long run, help the enterprise do a better job of delivering its products and services to the ultimate consumer. The organization becomes more flexible, able to analyze its products and processes with more insight, react to changes in the market, upgrade products and create more sizzle and value-added features to new and existing products.

The organization also is more apt to attract the type of employees who will help it sustain its growth and success. When Interim Services, a Fort Lauderdale-based temporary-staffing company, and Lou Harris & Associates asked 1,006 top-performing managers what kind of workplace they'd be reluctant to leave, nearly three-quarters cited organizations "that promoted fun and closer relationships with their colleagues." [14]

Understanding Customer Needs

How can you help ensure that your organization continues to deliver products and services in creative and innovative ways? How can you keep your associates motivated to focus on top-quality production? How can you make sure that you are adapting to the increasing needs of your customers?

The answer to these questions may be found in carefully minding the three key components that make up the products and services element:

1. Understanding our present and future customers and their needs
2. "Sharing and learning" throughout the organization
3. Using knowledge to make appropriate change

Your product and service offerings reflect the life of your organization. So it makes sense that at least once a year the leadership, along with associates and representative customers, should pause long enough to take a thoughtful look at how your products and services are satisfying the needs of both your external and internal customers.

Such a review includes probing questions like: Are your products and services doing a better job than your competitors to satisfy customers in

At least once a year the leadership, along with associates and representative customers, should pause long enough to take a thoughtful look at how your products and services are satisfying the needs of both your external and internal customers.

your market? Why are people buying your products or your services? Why are customers returning—or not—for your offerings?

This in-depth, customer-focused study assists every stakeholder in understanding and reinforcing the values that is providing the organization with its edge. What you learn in this rigorous process is grist also for building a motivated workplace culture that meets customer needs in a highly effective manner.

Change Teams

One effective way to make such a study work is to create change teams. Usually comprised of about ten members, these teams bring together representatives from all levels of the divisions or departments that will implement or be affected by the recommendations of the change team.

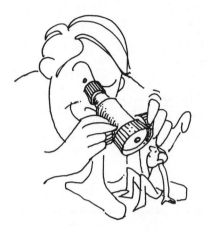

Change teams can be an organization's most useful critics.

The role of these teams is to act as if they comprise the organization's greatest critics. So the questions they raise focus on where the enterprise is strongest and where it is most vulnerable.

The team might discuss potential weaknesses in current product and service offerings or, even better, before new products hit the market. When defects are found, problems can be fixed before the marketplace forces it. This same change team may also be used to benchmark competitors' products, carefully scrutinizing them for weaknesses and strengths and then objectively comparing them to your products.

The output of this task group should be specific recommendations for change that will help the enterprise set priorities necessary to maintain its market strength or to push it ahead of the competition. The team's recommendations are made to the executives of the enterprise, possibly even to the board. A measure of the team's success is its ability to set aside parochial interests and put the interests of the entire enterprise first.

A subset of the change team also meets to analyze the relationships between stakeholders in different departments within the enterprise. For example, these smaller subcultural teams look at how the marketing department is serving the customer needs of stakeholders in the sales department. Sales might have suggestions that can help marketing improve the sales literature it produces to make the sales staff more productive when dealing with clients. This is a case of everyone in the enterprise asking a simple question: "How well am I serving my stakeholders both upstream and downstream?"

Specific questions that might focus a change team's discussion include:

- Do we know our customers today? What are their needs, wants and values?
- Who are our future customers? What will their needs, wants and values be?

- Are we doing better than our competitors at satisfying present customer needs?
- Are we delivering our products and services better than our competitors do?
- Do customers enjoy using our products and services?
- Do we respond well when our customers have questions or problems?
- How can we improve upon our product offerings today?
- What will make our products and services viable in the future?

These questions need to be answered for both external and internal customers, as they will lead to the changes that are required to make your organization and its offerings viable and adaptable to shifting markets.

Teaming up with several energetic external customers is a great way to make sure you understand your customers' needs, as well as to improve your current products and services. Sometimes we get complacent and stop at just being "good." But no organization can sustain itself by standing still. If you're not striving to lead, you're likely falling behind.

Also, addressing the needs of internal customers ensures continual fine-tuning of internal processes, employee coordination, empowerment, integration and teamwork, which builds a strong sense of involvement and makes success a natural outcome.

While the change team is intended to last indefinitely, the membership should be rotated periodically to give other associates the opportunity to bring up fresh ideas and approaches, and to share in this "leadership process."

Sharing and Learning

One of the best ways to stay competitive is to become an organization in which all the stakeholders are encouraged to find solutions to challenges. Creating opportunities for continual learning through on-site workshops, industry seminars, tuition-reimbursed university classes, or even rewards for personal improvement, pays dividends.

Membership on change teams provides learning opportunities. Other ways include open discussions between leaders and associates on pertinent and relevant topics in which associates are encouraged to provide input. One company has garnered national coverage for its policy of openly sharing financial information, as well as problems, with associates, who then take an active role in the resulting problem-solving opportunities.

Springfield Remanufacturing of Springfield, Missouri, rebuilds car and truck engines and sells them to auto, truck, and farm equipment manufacturers. Important clients include General Motors, Chrysler, Sears, Mercedes Benz, Navistar, and J.I. Case. Its story underscores the value of empowering associates.[15]

In 1983, the plant faced a shutdown until its parent organization, International Harvester, agreed to sell it to plant manager Jack Stack and a dozen employees. To survive, the company relied on its employees to keep up with the industry and the best products and services of its competitors. The company did better than survive. It has grown into a healthy organization, with 30 percent of its stock owned by employees.

A key ingredient of the company's success is its openness with associates. Weekly, the enterprise holds its "Great Game of Business." In these sessions, between 40 and 50 employees shout out their departments' weekly income and expense information while everyone jots it down. Representatives take this information back to their own departmental meetings where they share such important information as the company's cash flow, income statements and balance sheets with the rest of their colleagues. Employees embrace this information as a measurement of how well they are doing on a daily basis.

The company does not stop at sharing financial data. Employees give something in return. They are expected to spend one hundred hours a year in classes that range from seventh-grade reading and mathematics to statistical process control at all their plant sites. The focus on continuous education has paid off; approximately 90 percent of management positions are filled from within the company.

Springfield Remanufacturing is no IBM of the Missouri Ozarks. The company's assembling plants can get messy—workers tear down engines and put them back together. But the employees who rebuild those engines have a better than working knowledge of annual reports and financial statistics. They can use these statistics to measure their progress in the roles they perform and set their own goals. And they can relate those reports and statistics to their own jobs of making better products that satisfy the high demands of their clients.

But more than that, these employees are motivated to improve. They know working on an engine today will play a part in the company's success tomorrow. Studies have repeatedly demonstrated that employees develop strong loyalties to their employers when they know their organizations are investing in them, often through education and training programs that improve their skills and enhance their personal images.

The sense of openness and learning at Springfield Remanufacturing encourages an understanding of why certain changes in the organization are necessary. Knowing what's expected of them, employees are able to navigate change without being tossed into turmoil. In fact, the employees are a good source of information that can be tapped to identify, initiate and implement needed changes.

When you know your customers and how well your products and services are serving their needs, wants and values, you are in a strong position to make appropriate change.

Using Knowledge to Make Change

When you know your customers and how well your products and services are serving their needs, wants and values, you are in a strong position to make appropriate change.

Change in life is a given; change in business is a must. Making the right changes at the right time is the real challenge.

Armed with the honest appraisals that come out of change teams, or from regularly scheduled meetings with department heads and associates, insightful organizations have the ability to move quickly to improve existing products, or develop and launch new products, with the commitment of cooperative associates.

Often leaders of organizations must shift gears to maintain financial health or meet unexpected challenges from competitors. But when associates are informed of the direction of the organization and know their roles, such changes are less likely to result in suspicion of their leaders' motives. In fact, the employees themselves might already anticipate the need for needed change.

At Marion, the culture supported any associate who wanted to question the direction of the organization. And it was part of the core values that any leader would respond to the question respectfully. Information that is helpful has a way of building support and understanding. If it's a core value to fix problems before they affect the customer, then associates will see it as their duty to contribute to changes that support the enterprise.

When combined with incentives that reward associates for helping to implement changes in the least painful way, a sharing of customer satisfaction research findings can result in a powerful force toward greater success. An organization that serves its own colleagues as customers becomes a wellspring of innovation.

Cultural Conscience Checklist	Yes	No
• Do you have an ongoing process for analyzing your customers' (internal and external) needs, wants and values, today and for the future?		
• Do you have a defined, ongoing process for being as critical of your products and services as your most critical customer or your toughest competitors?		
• Does your organization involve customers in your product improvement or product development processes?		
• Does your organization share information concerning customer needs, problems and opportunities and operating results of the organization broadly and consistently?		
• Do your associates have confidence in your products today and in their ability to produce and launch new and better products in the future?		

CHAPTER 5

Direction: The Focus of the Organization

"Vision is the best manifestation of creative imagination and the primary motivation of human action. It's the ability to see beyond our present reality, to invent what does not yet exist, to become what we not yet are."

—Stephen R. Covey, A. Roger Merrill & Rebecca R. Merrill, Authors, *First Things First* [16]

Direction Element Defined:

The clear and focused path that provides purpose and vision for an enterprise, its subcultures and associates to plot meaningful strategies and tactics, goals and objectives for their organization.

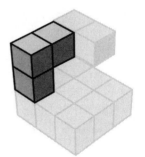

The Process:

- Clarify the purpose of our organization
- Establish a clear vision of our future state
- Create strategic initiative (three to ten years)
- Determine the tactics (one to three years)
- Set goals and objectives (this year)

Astute managers know that the quality of their organization's culture, reflected by how well it embraces a core of well-chosen values and cares for its internal and external stakeholders, drives its performance, productivity and profitability.

With these elements in place, savvy managers next want to ensure the sustained success and improvement of the enterprise by focusing on where it is headed or, better yet, the direction in which they want it to go.

Too often, organizations flounder because both the leaders and the employees lack a focus of where they want the enterprise to go. Even in organizations with sophisticated planning systems that benefit from clarity at the top, one can find associates at lower levels who have little or no understanding of the organization's direction and priorities.

Direction specifies the steps that an organization intends to take in order to continuously improve the way it meets the needs, wants and values of its customers, whether those customers are inside or outside the enterprise.

When you ask these people to describe the purpose for the organization, they shrug their shoulders and shake their heads. Too many managers assume their employees learn the direction and purpose of the organization by osmosis. That doesn't happen. The organization's purpose and direction must be crystal clear and effectively communicated.

Without a clear sense of direction, many employees "check their minds" in the parking lot, put in their eight hours and then leave for the "really important" activities in their lives. What a waste! We spend the majority of our waking hours at work. So workplaces should be positive environments where associates feel energized by what they achieve every day—and will achieve tomorrow, next week, by the end of this year and during their entire career.

Defining Direction

Direction specifies the steps that an organization intends to take in order to continuously improve the way it meets the needs, wants and values of its customers, whether those customers are inside or outside the enterprise. Indeed, setting your course for the future depends on knowing exactly who you want as your customers and what they can expect from you today and what they are going to expect tomorrow.

People in organizations that have a strong sense of direction can set sail like explorers who trust the accuracy of their compasses, knowing exactly where they are headed. They are prepared for the challenges that might lie ahead in their journey and know how to take advantage of the opportunities that present themselves.

Leaders of a branch, division or of the entire enterprise are responsible for applying the direction of the overarching culture to their own subculture, and involving the people who report to them in their own subcultural direction-setting process. We know from studies that the manager's behavior is the most powerful influence on the culture. People are never going to perform at, or even near, their best, without a clear sense of where they are going, and without the desire to help the enterprise get there.

There are five critical components to the direction element that allow leaders to address fundamental questions: "Why does this enterprise exist?" "Where are we going?" and "What's my role in this endeavor?"

- *Purpose:* States the organization's reason for being.
- *Vision:* Provides a clear picture of our future state.
- *Strategic Intent:* Develops the key steps to fulfill the organization's vision.
- *Tactics:* Breaks down strategic initiatives into intermediate steps to reach the strategic objectives.
- *Goals and Objectives:* Spell out specific team and individual assignments for the current year.

These components are most easily understood when they are simple and clear. They rarely require huge amounts of analysis. Nor do their explanations require large notebooks full of narrative and exposition. But they need to be appropriate strategically, communicated and kept in front of every associate daily, and continuously reinforced.

For workplace cultures to live up to their true potential, all associates must feel they are intregal parts of planning how their organization will get to that better place where they want it to go. If associates are expected to own their roles in making the organization successful, they must want to go where the organization is headed and understand their responsibilities and obligations for getting there.

Why? First, clarity of direction and involvement in achieving desired results satisfy a key human need to build relationships with others. Second, associates will be more likely to internalize the plans and subsequently carry them out because they are included in the planning and movement toward the more desirable future.

Stop and think about it. When people listen to what you have to say, don't you feel more valued? And when people understand what you are saying, don't they usually respond more positively? By listening closely and respectfully to your stakeholders and incorporating their thoughts into organizational plans, you are building a culture that encourages new ideas, true involvement, a sense of ownership, and the ability to identify issues and opportunities, and make appropriate changes. This makes for rich, fruitful planning, informed determination of priorities and dramatically improved execution and outcomes. This becomes a powerful process.

There are many planning tools and methods available, developed by academics, consultants, and business leaders. But they all start with sitting down as a team and asking: "Other than to make a profit, what is our real purpose for being?" That's the beginning. That's the defining moment of self-recognition.

Purpose

Profit is the by-product of successfully fulfilling one's business purpose. The purpose is what really defines the reason why the organization exists and why people come to work every day.

Consider prescription-drug maker Merck's decision in 1987 to give away Mectizan, a drug it developed to treat river blindness, a disease caused by a parasite common in African villages. Originally, the company planned to market the drug to third world governments and international relief organizations, but when it didn't make a profit, Merck CEO Dr. P. Roy Vagelos, a physician and scientist, decided to give away the medicine to the countries where the need was greatest.

His decision grew out of the company philosophy, expressed best by George W. Merck, the last member of the Merck family to head the company. He said: "Medicine is for patients. It is not for the profits. The profits follow, and if we have remembered that, they have never failed to appear. The better we have remembered it, the larger they have been."[17] Merck's purpose was to provide medicine to people who needed it. Simple and straightforward.

The purpose needs to be specific enough so that everyone clearly understands how it pertains to the enterprise but broad enough so that it can adapt to change or take advantage of new opportunities.

Your company's purpose should be "broad, fundamental, and enduring,"[18] as authors James C. Collins and Jerry I. Porras discuss in their book *Built to Last*. The authors suggest that leaders ask: "What would be lost if we ceased to be?" Collins and Porras assert that the purpose needs to include three key virtues:

1. The purpose of the organization must be broad enough to encompass the dynamics of the environment in which the organization operates.
2. The purpose must be fundamental enough so that it is rooted in the strengths of the organization as it is today or as it can be tomorrow.
3. The purpose of the organization must be enduring.

The purpose needs to be specific enough so that everyone clearly understands how it pertains to the enterprise but broad enough so that it can adapt to change or take advantage of new opportunities. This can be a balancing act. Consider the Kansas City Area Transportation Authority. In creating its purpose, or mission statement, the KCATA's executive team developed the following purpose statement:

"Develop, provide, manage and coordinate public transit options serving regional customers and constituencies in a safe, courteous, efficient and innovative manner."

This statement in part is an effort to move the authority away from its stodgy image as simply the local bus company to become a full-service transportation enterprise. The executive leadership team is trying to avoid the mistakes made by the railroads in not moving into other modes of transportation, such as trucking and air transport, which would have sustained their dominance in transportation.

Asking the simple question, "Are we in the bus business or are we in the transportation business," the KCATA's executive team launched a study of its purpose—its reason to exist. The future of metropolitan transportation in Kansas City envisions light rail, a contingent of smaller buses and vans that reach into neighborhoods, and an emphasis on tourism.

To the degree an organization can maintain a balance of defining its purpose so that it is well understood without limiting its opportunities, it can foster a more adaptable culture that will flourish today and endure tomorrow.

Consider the Walt Disney Company's purpose to "use our imaginations to bring happiness to millions," the Marriott Corporation's to "give friendly service to guests, provide good food at a fair price, and work hard to make a profit to create more jobs," or Hewlett-Packard's: "Making a contribution to society via electronic equipment for the advancement of science and the welfare of humanity."[19]

These purpose statements work because they are broad enough to allow their companies to navigate through changing economics and technologies, yet are fundamental enough to reflect their specific attributes and capabilities. They reflect each company's philosophy and reason for existing and are easily understood by every associate.

Test your own organization's purpose statement by asking:
- Does it state in simple terms the purpose of our organization (division, department or team)?

- Does it speak to our strengths and capabilities?
- Will it remain appropriate over time?
- Will it steer our strategic thinking and planning, and keep us focused?

If everyone in your organization cannot answer all of these questions in a positive manner, perhaps additional time and effort is required to sort through your organization's reason for being.

Vision

Vision, the second component of the direction element, is what your organization wants to look like five to ten years from now. Vision provides the inspiration that gives flight to your purpose by painting a picture of the better place where you want to take your organization.

The vision must not only inspire all stakeholders, it must also enable them to determine where they are on the journey by providing the means for measuring progress toward that vision. Ideally, it should quantify how great you desire the organization to be and provide a time frame for taking your enterprise to these new heights.

One organization I worked with crafted a well-intended vision statement that went something like this: "We are an exceptional (type of organization) with an inspired workforce providing superior regional service."

I challenged the leaders to tell me what the words "exceptional," "inspired" and "superior" meant to each of them. The words, it turned out, had so many meanings to so many people that they were all but empty of any real inspirational value.

I asked them to compare their present vision statement to the famous statement made by former President Kennedy when he reenergized our space program: "I believe this nation should commit itself to achieving the goal, before this decade is out, of landing a man on the moon and returning him safely to earth."[20]

At first, even the scientists at NASA thought this was a cockeyed dream. They had trouble getting even one rocket off the ground consistently, much less sending someone to the moon. But, as it turned out, when they buckled down and bought into the vision, it happened. And it happened within the time frame envisioned by Kennedy.

Any question about where Kennedy wanted us to go? To the moon. Any question about who was going? Our new heroic astronauts—and, in a sense, the entire nation. Any question about the time frame? In the next ten years.

This clear vision not only inspired the people at NASA, but the nation's families, workers and classrooms full of awed students. As Americans bought into this vision, the force of its intent and the resulting output of new technologies changed the world as the United States joined the space race. It was clearly the vision of a man who knew how to inspire people to greatness.

President Kennedy's statement is an example of an effective, working vision. It's believable, inspiring and quantifiable; progress could be measured at any time because the vision was so concrete.

Yet, too often vision statements are poorly conceived. Many are merely "dream statements" that will never be reached. Others are so long and complex that they complicate rather than clarify. More often than not, they fail to provide a way of measuring whether the enterprise is succeeding in its journey.

As author Joel Barker, author of *Paradigms*, puts it: "Vision without action is merely a dream. Action without vision just passes the time. Vision with action can change the world." [21]

Vision that is properly conceived, communicated and institutionalized can build excitement and direct action, leading to outstanding results and even greatness.

We need that hope, focus and energy a strong vision creates to maintain our enthusiasm and momentum. With a clear vision, we are more productive because we are part of a larger quest. As an organization you can do worse than to ask yourself: "Where's our moon? How soon are we going to get there?"

Vision provides the inspiration that gives flight to your purpose

Test your vision by asking:

- Is it clear where the vision will take us?
- Is it clear who is involved?
- Is it quantifiable?
- Is it possible?
- Does it inspire the intended stakeholders?

The overall organization needs a clear vision, but so does each subculture, if the organization as a whole is to fulfill its destiny.

To be effective, the vision must inspire people to greatness, and must be easily visualized, as well as measurable. Inspiration has to cause us to want to get to this better place where we have chosen to go.

Strategy

When an organization and its subcultures have a clear purpose and an inspiring vision, the next step is to devise a meaningful strategy that creates for the stakeholders a way to reach that vision. Strategic plans get a lot of attention for good reason. They provide focus and value for stakeholders and are essential to building an effective culture.

"Good planning is being able to determine where the barely submerged and strategically important rocks are in the roaring river of business, and then using them to cross successfully to the other side,"[22] former Marion Merrell Dow president and CEO Fred Lyons said many, many times. Identifying where the most important "rocks" lie is a critical part of any journey.

Depending on the industry, strategic plans should map out major steps over the next five to ten years.

Strategies spell out the large steps our enterprise needs to take to reach our destination. Closely linked substrategies must also be developed within each subculture. They may be as simple as the marketing department improving its relationship with sales to satisfy the needs of that department as well as to sell the product more effectively to the end user.

Once you've nailed down these strategic steps, determining the smaller, tactical steps is much less daunting. If you don't already have an internal strategic planning expert to help plot out these steps, it can be very productive to hire a well-qualified consultant, at least at the beginning.

Such facilitators generally are versed in different strategic planning models and are able to help select the most appropriate model for the particular size and type of organization. They are also able to involve both internal associates and outside stakeholders while objectively keeping the planning process on target. As professional planners, they often can tap into important external data and other resources.

Too often the value of strategic plans is based on the quantity rather than the quality of planning. A well-thought-out final plan should be no

> *A meaningful, organizational strategic plan outlines the major steps in the road map to the future and provides clarity for everyone.*

more than 10-15 pages long, excluding data and research findings. Remember, the plan's real purpose is to communicate the big steps necessary to achieve the organization's vision and to set the stage for the tactical plans and individual goals and objectives that follow.

A meaningful, organizational strategic plan outlines the major steps in the road map to the future and provides clarity for everyone. A good strategic plan not only provides guidance, it also builds confidence about the future.

Some good reasons for developing strategic plans include: the need to shift products from one technology to another; the development of a new product; and the need to make the shift to a new customer base or new markets.

Test your strategies by asking:
- Are the strategies appropriate for current and future customers?
- Can the strategies be quantified?
- Can the strategies be accomplished with the resources available to us?
- Are we in control of the resources required to fulfill the strategies?

Tactics

Tactics are the smaller steps that help us implement our larger strategies.

A tactical plan breaks each strategic initiative down into shorter, quantifiable steps that can be achieved in one to three years, and assigns responsibility for completing them. It's a process of finding what needs to be done, assigning tasks and determining the time frame for completion. The tactical plan also involves identifying the resources required to complete them in the time frame that is agreed upon during the annual planning process.

Tactical plans should be updated every year. Assume you are developing a new product or preparing to license, acquire, or launch a new product. The tactical plan outlines the individual steps, or tactics, that various departments will be called upon to perform, whether it's research, product development, deciding on a marketing plan or distributing the product.

In other words, an organization's tactical plans subdivide the strategies, establish realistic deadlines and determine departmental and team responsibilities for carrying out the plans. Each tactical plan should cover the critical steps needed to move the organization through each strategic milepost in the journey.

Test your tactical plans by asking:
- Is it clear how much will be accomplished?
- Is it clear which organization(s) will be responsible?
- Is it clear when it will be done?
- Is it clear how much it is going to cost?

Goals and Objectives

Once your tactics are pinned down, you are prepared to determine who is going to be responsible for each of those tactical initiatives that ultimately will be linked to the enterprise's overriding purpose and vision.

This is where you as a leader should be able to say, "Yes, if I do these things, we're going to accomplish the tactics that will get us closer to our vision." This exercise then results in objective, measurable goals and deadlines for teams and individuals.

This fifth and critical component of the direction element is where all of the other elements become operational and real.

In order for goals and objectives to be as effective as possible, every associate who will assume responsibility for them must be directly involved in their development and the measurements to go with them. Everyone ought to ask the question: "Is what I'm doing really helping our organization reach our vision?"

This needs to be both an individual and a group effort—to make sure associates understand their own goals and objectives and how they fit into the larger context.

Defining, setting and tracking goals does not have to be complicated. In my seminars, I use these five helpful steps:

- Establish the context and priority for each goal
- Describe each necessary task in a way that propels the effort forward
- Determine how each task will be measured
- Create a deadline for completing the task
- Establish what percentage of the goal was attained and specify rewards

The cultural power of this effort lies in its ability to provide associates with a means of linking themselves to the purpose and vision, providing focus and encouraging associate involvement in the direction of the organization. It also gives each individual a keen sense of how his or her goals and objectives fit into the enterprise as a whole. Finally, it provides each associate a basis for measuring performance. Goals must be tangible and measurements as objective as possible. That way associates can assess each positive step made during the year, applying measurements they helped choose.

At Marion Laboratories, we conceived and implemented an innovative but simple method of prioritizing, measuring and reporting goal accomplishments. The form we used allowed associates to see exactly what they needed to do to help reach the vision, and, at the same time, to individually measure how well they were doing. Thus, the form also created an equitable and objective way to reinforce an associate's contributions through rewards and bonus programs.

STRATEGIC CATEGORY	TACTICAL CATEGORY	PERFORMANCE GOAL	COMPLETE BY	ACCOMPLISHMENTS	VALUE FACTOR	% GOAL ATTAINED	VALUE POINTS
Profit Growth	Sales	Reach sales of $22mm for Calamity Jane Ointment	FY 2001	Reached sales of $27,330,000 (Objective measurement directly from operating reports)	25	124	31
	Scale-Up	Complete sales scale-up to 600 representatives	9-1-2001	All salespeople were hired and trained by 8-30-2001	25	100	25
	Expense Management	Manage sales and marketing expenses to less than 26% of total product sales ($69,500,000)	FY 2001	Controlled total expenses to a level of $64,000,000 (Objective measurement directly from operating reports)	15	108	16.2
Cultural Leadership	Values	Communicate, reinforce and enforce core values within sales and marketing	FY 2001	Values institutionalization during 2000 was very positive with numerous examples of efforts to communicate the core values and numerous direct and meaningful interventions to reinforce and enforce values within the organization. (Subjective review by self and direct supervisor)	15	100	15
Process Improvement	Change Management	Develop and implement a change team to represent sales and marketing to develop a set of priorities for the division	FY 2001	Developed the team including 6 associates from S&M, 2 from internal stakeholder organizations and 2 external customers. Team developed a list of 4 initiatives that were approved by the divisional executive team and will be included in the 2002 tactical plan.	20	100	20
				2001 Goals and Objectives results	100	–	107.2

Associate annual goals and objectives

The columns represented in Marion's form include:

Strategic Category - Ties the individual's goals and objectives to the strategic plan of the organization.

Tactical Category - Relates goals to the tactical element in the organization's overall plan.

Performance Goal - Includes a brief description of the goals and/or objectives.

Complete By - The date that the goals and/or objectives are to be completed.

Accomplishments - A brief statement listing the results achieved.

Value Factor - A numeric indication representing the weight of these goals and/or objectives as a percent of the total of 100 percent.

Percent Goal Attained - This can be a subjective evaluation or an objective calculation if there is a measurable result.

Value Points - The product of the value factor x % goal attained. May be more than 100 percent, as many bonus plans allow for greater than 100 percent payout. It can be used to determine the percentage of bonus in cases where the results are lower than planned.

Goals were established before the beginning of each fiscal year, and then reviewed and, if necessary, modified, changed or replaced on a quarterly basis. Changes were easy to make and document. For example, anyone wishing to do so simply put a new goal into the goal sheets by adding a text box, or crossing out goals that were no longer valid.

To make this effort meaningful, associates should be engaged in setting their own goals. I have witnessed many situations where associates were willing to assume much higher goals, and even tougher measurements, than their managers would have set for them if working without the associates' input.

To help ensure that associates are meeting or exceeding their goals, they need to receive timely feedback. Reviews provide an opportune time for giving positive feedback, coaching, counseling, reassessing goals and/or revising objectives. No associate should have to wait longer than a quarter before an informal or formal review is conducted. Frequent informal reviews make the more formal annual performance reviews easier on both supervisors and associates.

Dealing with the Difficulties of Planning and Forecasting Accuracy

An ability to plan and forecast results effectively is necessary for leaders who want to set meaningful and measurable goals and objectives for the organization.

This was a major dilemma at Marion, as we tried to predict how well a new pharmaceutical product would do in the market. To deal with the challenges of forecasting in a way that made it more proactive and less reactive, we developed a three-pronged planning and measurement system called Sure-Probable-Possible Planning.

The first, or "sure," scenario projected conservative sales and earnings we assumed we could realize even if things went wrong, such as a Food and Drug Administration delay in approving a new product or a product claim for an existing product.

The second, or "probable," scenario projected the most realistic sales and earnings, with modest risks, that we could expect, given what we knew about the marketplace, our competitors and our customers.

The third, or "possible," scenario forecasts potentially higher sales and earnings we might expect if everything went very well, if our product was a hit with doctors and patients and we knocked the stuffing out of our competitors.

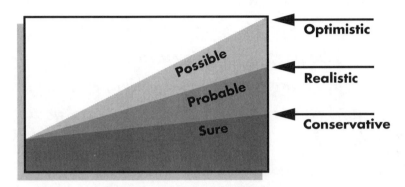

Sure–probable–possible planning

The benefit of this three-pronged forecast is that it allowed us to budget, plan and prepare for three eventualities. It allowed us to deal intelligently with those difficult variables: How many people will we need? How much advertising should we plan? What will be our biggest capital and expense issues?

Each unit within Marion matched its forecasts to these three scenarios. As a result, as the year progressed, we could determine where we were with regard to each forecast and readily adjust to budget for the year's performance, whether it was a big winner or a modest gain.

Sometimes we would find at mid-year that our performance was so far above the "possible" scenario that we would add more sales representatives and buy more advertising to drive our sales even higher.

The opposite was also true sometimes. If we learned that we weren't going to do as well as we expected, we could quickly revert back to a more modest plan, and cut back on hiring, new equipment and promotional spending. The important thing is that the preparation and measurements were in place because we had already planned and accounted for multiple scenarios.

This approach to forecasting also benefited associates, who were better able to anticipate their workload and respond to changes in plans and budgets. Further, because they were aware of how their own position and the overall organization might be affected, they were motivated to reach a higher level of performance.

The purpose of this cultural concept of pursuing a purpose, a vision, direction and values is to ensure that people know where they are in relation to their individual and collective objectives.

With this kind of planning, the organization is prepared to make appropriate adjustments rather than being caught by surprise. Management is less likely to make snap judgments at mid-year to lay people off or to be forced to take other difficult actions.

Remember, the purpose of this cultural concept of pursuing a purpose, a vision, direction and values is to ensure that people know where they are in relation to their individual and collective objectives. It's at the heart of cultural renewal.

As you work through the direction-setting process, keep the following components clearly in mind:

- The purpose clearly defines the organization's reason for being.
- The vision inspires excitement about a quantifiable event in the future.
- The strategy specifies the big steps toward your vision, emphasizing your strengths and minimizing weaknesses.
- The tactics address who will do what, by when, how and how much.
- The goals and objectives spell out specific assignments and expectations.

These components become crucial in building momentum for your culture as you propel your enterprise toward its desired destination. As you meld the direction of the organization with its core values and the quality of its products and services, you will set the stage for a tangible improvement in performance and overall cultural effectiveness.

As leaders, you can't do this alone. As described earlier, to engage your associates in developing a strong, adaptive culture requires a knowledge-based approach, in which associates can expand their skills. They may need to be coached through these processes. And they will certainly need encouragement to try new methods and to explore innovative ways to overcome challenges.

It is crucial, then, for emerging cultural leaders to fully and regularly communicate the organization's purpose, vision and strategy to their associates, much as President Kennedy pushed a nation forward with his vision of going to the moon and back. Helping associates to understand their role in the culture will encourage them to identify with the direction the enterprise is going and to make its destination their own.

The result will be increased job performance, acceptance of responsibility, lower turnover and absenteeism, and higher morale, which translates into higher productivity and greater profitability—a culture that pays.

Cultural Conscience Checklist	Yes	No
• Does your organization have a clearly stated purpose that every associate can state with total understanding and commitment?		
• Does your organization have a clearly defined vision statement that inspires each associate to fulfill its purpose?		
• Do you have a strategy for taking your culture or subculture where you want it to go?		
• Do you develop and implement tactical plans for your organization that can be completed in one to three years using meaningful action steps?		
• Do your leaders, teams and associates have specific and measurable goals and objectives that they helped choose?		

CHAPTER 6

Structure: Who's Responsible for What?

"The bigger you get, the harder you must continually fight back the bureaucracy and preserve entrepreneurial spirit."

—Herb Kelleher, CEO Southwest Airlines [23]

Structure Element Defined:

Provides clarity about what has to be done in the organization and who is responsible for getting it done, while affording the associates a deep sense of ownership of the processes used to accomplish their work.

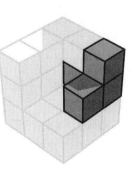

The Process:

- Ensure organizational capacity to achieve our goals and objectives
- Evaluate and update our policies and procedures
- Establish ownership and commitment to get the most out of our operating processes
- Develop effective cultural processes to meet our cultural enhancement goals

When people talk about the structure of an organization, whether it's a business, a country club or a charitable foundation, they most often refer first to the basic organizational chart.

Loosely described, the structure element describes who is responsible for what and how things get done. So, we might assume that with the right structure, and the right people in the right jobs, we will to be able to carry out the goals and objectives that allow us to effectively serve the needs, wants and values of our customers.

But, remember, we want our cultures to have a clear sense of where they're going and how they are going to get there. We want leaders who aren't afraid of change and who have a keen desire to inspire dynamic organizations that can continually accommodate the changing needs, wants and values of their customers and other stakeholders.

If one of the objectives is to be more productive, and ultimately more profitable, the question for the enterprise is more than, "Who has the power to do things?" Designing a structure that nurtures a strong, adaptive culture, in which overarching beliefs and common values are greater than self-interest, requires asking the larger question: "How do we harness the power of our individual and collective human resources to maximize the potential of the organization?"

Viewed this way, we can begin to integrate structure into our cultural journey of continuous improvement and innovative change, taking into account how we orient associates, promote positive decision-making and organizational learning and prepare for the succession of leadership.

When you take apart the structure element, you are basically considering three essential areas of interest:

1. The organizational components that comprise the principal building blocks
2. The policies and procedures that allow you to bring order and discipline to your organization
3. The processes that include not only those that are used to produce the output of the enterprise but also those cultural processes that continuously build and reinforce your organizational culture

Whether you are a chief executive officer or a division or department head, it is part of your job to help create a structure that can carry your enterprise to your destination. You may have been with the organization for years or perhaps you just walked in the door. But no matter what your situation is, the way your structure integrates culture is key to the sustained success of your organization.

Organization Design: The Components

This book is not intended to be an in-depth study of organizational design, but it bears discussing because of its importance to understanding effective work cultures. As a leader, one of your most important duties is to ensure that associates within the organization are aligned in a way that allows them to work together effectively.

Consider Southwest Airlines' team-oriented approach to empowering its associates. Southwest is more than the sum of its airplanes, maintenance teams and flight crews. It has an overriding mission to provide low fares and efficient service to its passengers, many of whom might not otherwise be able to travel by air. The ground crews, gate agents and cabin attendants all embrace their individual roles in making sure a plane full of satisfied passengers takes off on time, knowing planes make money in the air, not when marooned on the ground.

When Peg C. Neuhauser, co-author of *Culture.Com: Building Corporate Culture in the Connected Workplace*, asked Linda Rutherford, senior manager of public relations for Southwest Airlines, to describe the airline's secret for being able to rapidly deliver new services, Rutherford responded that Southwest distinguishes itself with a structure that nurtures people who share "high energy, altruism, dedication and loyalty to the cause that is Southwest."[24]

Defining Basic Structures

The most common organizational designs include: conventional hierarchical structures, matrix management and team-based systems.

Hierarchical structures are traditional, top-down systems, with a chief executive perched at the top and a chain of command stretching to the lowest associate. These organizations often reflect the cultural values of the top executive. The challenge here is to avoid a structure that results in dependency on upper management, who end up making decisions in reaction to crises, as if they were constantly putting out fires.

Allowing leaders in subcultures to have more autonomy and authority to make decisions will result in a structure that plays to the strengths of their personalities and the personalities of their divisions or branches. It is my experience that leaders who are given responsibility willingly take on more, thereby increasing profitability. Also, encouraging leaders to think for themselves results in a strong gene pool when the time comes for choosing future leaders of the enterprise.

In a *matrix organization*, executives split leadership. One set leads the day-to-day administrative site management while the other leads and directs the overall functions of departments or divisions within an enterprise.

> *Allowing leaders in subcultures to have more autonomy and authority to make decisions will result in a structure that plays to the strengths of their personalities and the personalities of their divisions or branches.*

This results in associates working across multiple subcultures. For example, associates in manufacturing may work together as a global manu-facturing team while, at the same time, the team members also answer to a separate administrative organization back at their specific work locations. Each organization can and does have its own unique culture. The two individual cultures can flourish and even nourish each other when they share overarching enterprise-wide values and a sense of moving in the same direction to accomplish a mutual purpose and vision.

Team-based systems have a flatter management. Individuals are expected to carry out their responsibilities within a group dynamic, rather than serving the expectations of a supervisor in a hierarchical, top-down operation.

To be effective these systems require effective communication and a lot of trust. Flattened forms of management also rely on lots of training to ensure that team members and their leaders know how to build subcultures that support the organization's overarching goals and objectives.

Many organizations choose to develop hybrids of these three main types of structures. For example, teams may be formed long term for standing projects or on a shorter basis for short-term projects in any of the organizational models. The most successful teams have been shown to develop goals, objectives and timetables. This gets everyone on the same page with a true sense of teamwork and ownership in the outcomes.

When Hewlett-Packard executives saw the need to shorten the computer company's product delivery time, managers Mei-Lin Cheng and Julie Anderson devised a team approach to tackle the problem. Promising their bosses they would complete the project in nine months, the two pulled together a team of 35 staff members.[25]

Cheng and Anderson spelled out the project's goals and the ground rules, but nothing more, intentionally seeking to empower the team by giving it the autonomy to come up with its own solutions. Instead of becoming lost and confused, the staff members in nine months came up with specific recommendations to solve the company's slow distribution problem.

Given autonomy, the team members were challenged to take the initiative, acting mainly on their own ideas, rather than being handed down someone else's. They found ways to cut the average delivery time from 26 days to 8 days. Though guided by project managers, the team pulled off this feat with little direct instruction.

Relating Organizational Design to Culture

An effective structure that nurtures a strong, adaptive culture requires a clear and logical assignment of responsibilities that promote autonomy, innovation and a sense of locality. People desire close relationships, not just with their customers but also with the leaders and organizational divisions to which they report. Without such relationships, it's difficult to develop trust and respect.

One of the best ways to fire up your associates is to show them that a positive relationship with their supervisor or manager will assist their own success. Interference with these local relationships can disrupt them by robbing them of autonomy and self-initiative.

Consider Xerox, which has struggled incessantly in recent years to recreate and reorganize itself into a vital, dynamic, growing company again. At one time Xerox had over 75 focused local branches that exercised a tremendous amount of autonomy. They were very efficient in meeting the needs of their local markets. However, one of the challenges for the company was that many of the largest, and most profitable, customers were national organizations. So, Xerox leadership shuffled its organizational structure in an effort to cater to these national organizations. Sales and marketing became more centralized, but as a result the branches lost much of their identity as strong local subcultures.

Is there absolute clarity about who is responsible for what in your organization? Are you free of duplication of responsibilities?

Another result was confusion over who was accountable to whom. Some people came to work focused only on the national accounts while others showed up to work only on the local accounts, resulting in a diffused sense of accountability. The people in the branches had difficulty taking the same ownership for the national accounts as they once did for their former local accounts, which were coincidentally branches or divisions of national organizations. It became difficult to retain a consistent sales and servicing commitment to both the national and local accounts. Even large customers were confused. In the past, local decision makers of large national accounts had dealt with local sales representatives. Now, they might have to deal with a national account manager in some other location as their primary contact.

As a result, it took a lot more people than Xerox's top management originally had thought to effectively service these national accounts. There was a bureaucratic overlay of redundant responsibilities. The former bonds between local sales reps and their local customer contacts loosened, service diminished and sales began to sag. This diffused method of servicing national accounts often results in a need for more people, more travel and fewer close relationships.

Customers are much happier, and most often better served, when they have a close working relationship with their sales and service contacts. With today's technology those relationships don't have to be local but they do need to be as personal as possible.

This doesn't mean you shouldn't assign someone to oversee and coordinate national accounts. But you need to create in the local branch a sense of responsibility and ownership toward all accounts, whether local or national. You want that branch manager to be as concerned about servicing a local General Motors or Procter & Gamble facility as anyone else in the country. You want that branch team looking for every sales opportunity in that geographic area.

So, right off the bat, as a cultural leader, you have to ask: Is there absolute clarity about who is responsible for what in your organization? Are you free of duplication of responsibilities? Are you staffed with people who are qualified to carry out the duties, objectives and responsibilities demanded to pursue your organization's crucial mission?

So here we are relating organizational design to the nurturing of culture. Once you can do that, you are ready for the next pieces of the structure element: policies and procedures.

Policies and Procedures

Policies and procedures are the rules of the road. If the structure is strengthened with creative personalities who take ownership of their responsibilities, they will more likely have the ability and desire to carry out the appropriate policies and procedures.

Appropriate organizational policies and procedures help create a pattern for success. Once consistent values are in place and the direction is set, an organization actually needs fewer rules and regulations. Too many rules, we all know, can be stifling. But carefully thought-out policies can act as guidelines and pathways that provide clarity when they are enforced. Without enforcement the policies become a mockery and carry little weight. In fact, they can become barriers to success.

Clear and effectively communicated policies and procedures:
- Help the organization meet its objectives
- Have a consistent impact on all stakeholders of the organization
- Clarify and support the values, goals and objectives of the organization

- Can be reviewed, updated, modified or replaced without causing disruption
- Are reinforced and enforced by every leader and associate

In my work with organizations, I usually find that policies and procedures are in place. But often they are either not enforced or are not enforced uniformly across every subculture. It's not surprising that people ignore policies that carry little or no consequence. They are empty of purpose and meaning.

Inappropriate policies and procedures prompt confusion and resentment among the stakeholders of the organization. Appropriateness, clarity and consistency are very important. If you have a policy, enforce it or eliminate it. If you say that you have a dress code and it's important that people look a particular way to carry out the operation of your organization, then enforce that dress code. Otherwise, you are sending a message to your associates that your policies and procedures are not important.

Polices and procedures are the necessary boundaries and guidelines for how we operate in the organization. They give us something tangible to measure our behavior against so that we act appropriately and with the necessary discipline to do our jobs and to respect the people with whom we work. If one of our core values is respect for each and every associate, then our policies and procedures must reflect that. Together, policies and procedures communicate to new hires, and to all associates for that matter, the best way to get along, to contribute to and to succeed in our enterprise.

Effective Operating and Cultural Processes

Every organization has two types of complementary processes at work: *operating processes* and *cultural processes*. Each type is crucial to the organization's long-term success.

While the two sometimes overlap, operating processes are used to carry out the day-to-day operational activities, while the cultural processes influence how associates learn about the organization and its culture and how they operate within it. We are most concerned here with cultural processes, but they need to be seen in relation to operating processes.

Operating Processes

The operating processes are the lifeblood of the organization. They allow us to meet our responsibilities, to get things done. Operating processes are how we provide our services, sell our products—how we deal with our customers.

They provide operating frameworks for development, manufacturing, accounting, marketing and sales, and financing and administration. How effective the processes are in collectively serving the "business of the enterprise" has a large bearing on how effective the culture will be in reaching its individual and collective objectives. To succeed, associates must feel a strong sense of ownership for the processes they are responsible for. This prevents creating "a place to hide" from the need to help and support others.

You create ownership when people feel they have input into the development and improvement of the processes. When you can create this collective "process ownership," you create a culture or subculture in which every stakeholder feels it is his or her role to make sure the enterprise succeeds.

For example, if we can create a culture in which associates working on the manufacturing floor have a feeling of ownership for the drills and presses they work with every day, they will take more responsibility for looking for new ways to improve their own operating processes. Ownership plants the seed of pride and personal commitment that reinforces the responsibilities that have been given to associates.

When people have input into the process, they take ownership of success

Too often, people feel forced to carry out processes invented or developed by someone else, even if they know that they could create a better way if only they were asked. Based upon my observations, a vast number of people in many of our organizations today lack any sense of involvement or ownership.

At TWA, for example, even long before the sale to American Airlines, there was a debilitating disconnect between the management and the employees, even though it was an employee-owned airline. Rather than embrace the responsibilities that come with ownership, many employees relied on the union to represent them in their relationship with management. As a result, the employees never got to a point where they acted like real owners, unlike at Southwest Airlines, where both the employees and their union representatives are inspired by a deep sense of pride.

So even though TWA employees were owners in name, in practice neither they nor their union representation felt committed enough to work together with management to make the airline operate as effectively as it could have. Tension resulted as individual employees suspected that they were doing their share, but others weren't reciprocating.

Gradually, a feeling of resentment prompted many to do only what was absolutely necessary. As you might expect, the outcome was that the entire airline operated at lower efficiency. TWA was unable to maintain consistency as it tried to carry out its objectives of on-time flights, expert baggage handling and helpful customer service.

When organizations fail to motivate employees to feel a sense of ownership, the employees no longer share management's vision and balk at changes they suspect are a subterfuge for management to get more out of them without giving anything back.

That is why leadership has to include associates in the planning, goal setting, measurement determination and implementation processes. The reward is that associates who take ownership will assume more responsibilities, because they know deep down that the process they are involved in not only reflects the enterprise's success, but their own success as well.

At Marion Laboratories associates in the Sale Support Center were mainly responsible for answering sales representatives' computer-based questions and solving software and hardware problems. But they also took responsibility for maintaining the systems and processes used. These associates prided themselves on their speed of service and the lack of recalls required to resolve problems.

As you look at all the operating processes that your organization encompasses, are you satisfied they are as good as they can be?

When your organization is producing steadily improving results and you are satisfied that the people in your area of responsibility have a keen sense of pride and ownership concerning their operating processes, you are ready to confront the challenges and opportunities that separate high-performance organizations from the masses.

At least eight key cultural processes exist that will invigorate, inform and sustain an organization: orientation, training and development, communication, decision-making, problem solving, organizational learning, change management and succession planning.

Cultural Processes

You might think of the cultural processes as the threads that weave together the cultural fabric of the enterprise or your own subculture. At first blush, cultural processes appear to be less tangible than operational processes, and thus more vulnerable to being overlooked, if not ignored, as niceties that don't make instant or concrete contributions to the bottom line.

The truth is that they are essential to ensuring the efficiency, productivity, adaptability and profitability of the organization over the long haul. Imagine a military battalion that has all the necessary gear but isn't oriented to the field, can't communicate adequately, makes incorrect decisions and, when lost, doesn't know how to read a compass, doesn't have the slightest idea where it's been or where it's going and has no plan to replace its leadership, should it become necessary in the thick of a battle.

At least eight key cultural processes exist that will invigorate, inform and sustain an organization: orientation, training and development, communication, decision-making, problem solving, organizational learning, change management and succession planning. While they sometimes overlap, they can be examined separately.

Orientation. An orientation process ought to provide every new employee with a true sense of the core values, purpose, vision, objectives and strategies of the organization. However, most organizations lack a formalized orientation method or process. New associates are many times sent to Human Resources to collect their health and insurance forms. Then they are expected to go to work and somehow pick up everything else they need to know about the organization on their own.

What usually happens is that they pick up most of their information in the lunchroom or at the water cooler. And a lot of that information isn't useful. This "informal orientation" may rely on a fellow associate who is well intentioned but misinformed. Or a disgruntled employee or "ring-leader" can give a recruit perverse ideas about the organization. How can you expect associates to gain the kind of focus and sense of involvement that results in organizational pride if you don't show them what you are trying to do with your organization and how their role fits with everyone else's?

Orientation should include a clear discussion of core values; the purpose and vision of the enterprise and its subcultures; the organization's goals and objectives; a description of the structure and the various operational responsibilities; an understanding of measurements and rewards; how decisions are made; and the kind of problem solving used by the organization to ensure peaceful and positive resolution of issues. This is also an ideal time to openly discuss the challenges and opportunities the organization is facing and how you are dealing with them.

Orientations don't have to be one-time meetings. They can consist of a series of sessions over a period of time, so that new employees can compare their actual experiences on the job with what is presented and discussed in the orientation process and ask for clarification if needed.

One useful idea is to hold a series of luncheons and orientation meetings on successive Fridays for the first six weeks of employment. Officers from different parts of the organization can present their area of responsibility and lead a discussion of the company, its values and its direction. These gatherings enable two-way exchange that is beneficial for both the new employees and the leadership.

Training and Development. Investment in training helps build technical skills and demonstrates your organization's commitment to associates' success. It provides your associates with a sense that they are being given the skills to grow in their jobs and advance in their careers.

Often associates are trained too generally. Associates will claim a greater ownership in a job in which they receive specific training to raise their pertinent skill levels. This includes seminars and classroom education that focus on new techniques and technologies related to present and future responsibilities. It might also include pairing the person with a mentor or with a coach who can help bring out new talents or help an associate work through mistakes.

Training leads to confidence, and as their skills improve, associates can be empowered to take greater responsibility for their roles and the processes in which they are involved. They develop feelings of pride that make coming to work an energizing event rather than a mind-numbing necessity. To sustain a high-performance culture associates need the opportunity to continually expand the skills and knowledge that allow them to meet and exceed the organization's expectations of what it hopes to achieve and where it wants to go. Appropriate training also demonstrates commitment to associates by investing in them and their future.

Communication. Most organizational problems grow from poor communication. Therefore, the goal is to have ongoing communication between all associates using a variety of media. Share the earnings increase and other good news. Explain where the company has to strengthen its objectives. Such open exchange builds trust.

Sponsor events to update stakeholders on where the company is headed, how it is going to get there, and how well it is doing in getting there. Treat these events as progress reports, and use them to celebrate company, team and individual successes.

At Marion, we conducted "Marion-on-the-Move" sessions several times a year. When the company became so large that the 2,600 Kansas City associates couldn't fit into a company facility, we all climbed onto school buses and traveled to the Municipal Auditorium in downtown Kansas City, Missouri. During these meetings, we celebrated our collective, team and individual successes. We also learned how we were doing financially that year and how we thought we would do the next year. Jim McGraw, COO, and other leaders often sat on a stool and casually answered questions from the company associates in a "town hall" format that brought the leaders much closer to the people and gave the associates an opportunity to interact with them in a warm and open manner.

We would also get an update on our benefit plans, and we could often expect to hear of some new perk. The meeting usually ended with an emotional, positive message from company founder, Ewing Kauffman. We would then all get back on the buses and eat a box lunch during the drive back to work. That might seem like a lot of warm fuzzies, but the "Marion-on-the-Move" rallies played an important role in nurturing our culture.

As I consult with leaders, I find that many are afraid or unable to communicate with associates at every level of the organization. The larger the organization, the more complex the problem. By centralizing a limited number of communications efforts during the year, the top management has an opportunity to talk directly with and even listen to every level of the organization.

These efforts ensure that a consistent message is shared. Studies suggest that the manager is the biggest single influence on the work culture. If that is true, the behavior and values communicated by the manager are certain to be mirrored by a large number of associates. Good communication at every level is an important component of the structural element of the Visionomics model.

Decision-Making. Related to the cultural training process is the effort to coach everyone in the enterprise to make wiser and more insightful decisions. I am still surprised at how little effort is put into training associates or leaders in the art and science of decision-making. Few leaders I speak to, train or consult with have ever received any training on the subject. In addition, very few organizations are even attempting to put in place a consistent model for decision-making within their enterprises.

A model for decision-making that has proven successful at a number of top organizations is a process called "Balanced Decision Making."[26] Leaders trained in this system are expected to use it frequently and to train their reports to use it as well.

The concept is intended to cause any decision maker to take into consideration the impact of a decision on all the stakeholders. Your responsibility is to let associates and organizations most affected by your decision know before you finalize and implement it. This allows people to know a decision is coming, and gives them an opportunity to prepare in a positive way. If they have a reason to believe the impact of a given decision is negative, they can choose to make the decision maker aware of that as well.

At first blush, the balanced decision-making process may seem somewhat bureaucratic. As it plays out, however, it actually saves time, because it avoids decisions that have to be rescinded later because they were ill conceived. The process also reflects an important core value when the organization believes that everyone has a right to be heard.

Problem Solving. While differences are best settled between associates, or between associates and their immediate supervisor, sometimes that's not possible. So people need to be able to work up the ladder of authority with their dispute or unsettled differences.

The key is to go up the ladder with the supervisor's full understanding and support. One way to make this work is to allow a grievance to rise up the chain of command until the matter is fully aired, allowing the problem to be solved at the lowest level possible. This process can go on until the parties resolve the issue, even if it means going to the chief executive officer's office.

Organizational Learning. To keep growing, an organization must remain competitive. Many books and articles have been written on ways to institutionalize the organizational learning process. The best note the ability of adaptive cultures to pass on knowledge and skills from the most talented associates to the associates who will follow them.

This philosophy allows your organization to keep its edge, as associates claim entrepreneurial ownership in sustaining the enterprise's competitiveness and tackling market changes with fresh and innovative ideas. By institutionalizing organizational learning through the free flow of ideas, encouragement of risks, balanced decision-making and sharing new skills, you create a reservoir of intellectual power.

These benefits extend to your customers. While many organizations claim to be customer-focused, how often is customer information shared with others in the organization and then systematically used to create appropriate change?

One strong way to institutionalize organizational learning is by employing change teams, as discussed earlier. These teams of employees challenge members of the organization to objectively assess how they are meeting their customers' needs, wants and values, and to share that knowledge across all subcultures of the enterprise. Provided on a regular basis, such knowledge can guide the enterprise forward to new opportunities at every level.

Change Management. Organizational learning may be compared to being on a space ship to the moon. We should feel fully confident that our space ship is as effective as any other space ship in the universe. So we need to develop a method to constantly evaluate our progress, and our ability to adapt to the challenges of the journey.

Our first priority is to be broadly aware of our customers' present and future needs, wants and values. Cultural leaders in the enterprise must ask themselves, are we customer-focused? Are we communicating to our associates where we are headed, and are we making decisions within the context of our purpose and mission?

And finally, are we taking full advantage of the knowledge gained from our relationships, learning from it and using it to make appropriate change?

This is how we use our change teams—to say what we are strong at and what we need to make stronger. In *Built to Last*, authors Collins and Porras underscore the need to formalize this change process. They note how a team of associates can be brought together from subcultures to scrutinize their organization's products and services, much as a serious competitor might.

By looking at your culture as a competitor might, you create a distance that fosters a more objective and less forgiving examination. That way you can put real teeth into this process of finding ways to make your culture pay.

Succession Planning. No leader remains forever. Succession is a challenge that is faced by every organization, large or small. So it stands to reason that every forward-looking organization needs an effective succession plan in order to sustain itself.

When you look at the very best cultures in American business, they all tend to have one thing in common—they promote from within whenever and wherever possible. For example, General Electric wouldn't think of going outside the company to recruit a new chief executive officer.

Yet, other companies that have struggled for years to reinvent or reorganize their floundering cultures constantly go outside to look for a magician to solve their internal problems. As a result, you see a lot of preventable failures due to the introduction of new leadership style and methods that are not suited to the culture of the enterprise.

To maintain a strong, adaptive culture, the most consistently successful organizations, as a rule, bring leaders up through the ranks. This is the best way to ensure that the new leader understands the organization's overarching beliefs and values and can relate to the subcultures throughout the enterprise.

But succession planning carries an inherent responsibility. You have to find the raw material and you have to make sure that potential cultural leaders are getting the kind of experience and training they need to rise to the next level of responsibility. That process itself requires a strong commitment. Therefore, this type of planning has to be formalized to create a pool of talented, future leaders who are dedicated to the culture, understand its values and are committed to its long-term success.

Leaders naturally spend a great deal of time working to improve the "operating processes" of their organizations, because these are the most obvious. As a result, often too little time is spent on the "cultural processes" that have a direct effect on the long-term success of the organization and its ability to serve its stakeholders.

As mentioned in the introduction, I like to refer to this dichotomy as working "in the house" rather than "on the house." Too often we are so task-oriented that we busy ourselves working on the mechanics inside our organization without stepping back to see how the integrity of the entire structure is responding to the environment in which it competes.

By becoming more cognizant of how the cultural processes affect the organization's overall operations, and holding leaders accountable for them, you are strengthening the entire structure of your organization, from the outside in. Every stakeholder benefits from the increased productivity, flexibility, autonomy, empowerment and improved outcomes. Associates feel they are rewarded for contributing fresh ideas and honing their skills. Customers see an organization committed to adapting to their needs, wants and values.

Though largely invisible, the cultural goals and objectives are enforced daily as leaders reflect and communicate the desired values and behaviors. And the organization's purpose and vision are in sync with the production and delivery of its products and services.

Cultural Conscience Checklist	Yes	No
• Are department and division responsibilities clear to everyone who needs to understand them?		
• Do you have an effective orientation process in place that is being consistently executed?		
• Are operating processes as effective as they can be?		
• Is every critical role filled with a competent associate, who fits both the job and the culture?		
• Are appropriate policies and procedures in place and operating effectively?		
• Are appropriate cultural processes in place and functioning well?		

CHAPTER 7

Measurements: Monitoring Our Progress

"Managers without performance measures for their areas of responsibility are like travelers without a map, pilots flying blind, or doctors without a stethoscope—they are working harder and accomplishing less than they otherwise could."

—Will Kaydos
Author, *Measuring, Managing, and Maximizing Performance* [27]

Measurements Element Defined:

Provides a means for timely feedback on the progress made by the organization and individual associates toward agreed-upon goals and objectives.

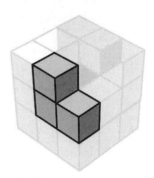

The Process:

- Ensure that we are measuring the right things
- Check that we are using the correct measurement methods
- Involve associates in setting goals and developing measurement processes
- Provide positive and timely feedback to associates

Measurements give us a reading on how close we are to reaching our goals and objectives. They enable people to focus their efforts, monitor their progress and create systems for accountability and rewards. In business, measurements also provide valuable milestones that show how well we are meeting our customers' needs, wants and values.

In a cultural sense, measurements both mirror and satisfy a powerful human need to see where we stand in relationship to others and to the better place where we want to be. For most of us, this need asserts its power in our lives, our spiritual growth, our careers and in the organizations to which we belong or for which we work. Healthy human beings aspire to do better, whether to increase our capacity for knowledge, perform athletic feats or excel in our careers and community service in a way that gains approval. We like to be part of a winning team even if it is as a fan.

Everyone wants to know the score

How would you like to attend a basketball game where no one kept score, or watch a golf tournament without knowing the players' standings? Not much point is there? Not much fun either.

The need to measure up manifests itself in the games we play, in our desire to belong and in our drive to succeed. So it amazes me to hear someone say, "I don't need to be measured, I know my job." That's like saying, "I don't need food, I never get hungry."

We rely on measurements every day. We want to know how long it takes to drive to work, how much money we have in our checking account and how well we are doing in our golf game or in our bowling league. Measurements allow us to celebrate our personal and group accomplishments, like losing a few extra pounds or achieving our team's monthly quota.

A good measuring system helps people perform even better. If we are rocketing to the moon, it's crucial to know how far we've gone, that we are on course and moving at the correct speed. If we are off course, we'd better have the tools necessary to make the appropriate adjustments to get back on course.

In an organizational culture, measurements can help us see if we are succeeding or not, so we can assess rewards or take corrective actions. In that sense, measurements provide focus for organizations and the people inside them, bringing discipline and order to this journey toward cultural renewal.

Unfortunately, managers too often use measurements as a club or a whip in an attempt to force employees to work harder or produce more. Employed in a positive way, measurement methods can be used to engage associates in setting higher goals for themselves and to find ways to produce more of what they really want to produce. Motivated associates often set higher goals and more stringent measures for themselves than their leaders are comfortable in setting for them.

In an ideal culture, every individual would have specific, attainable goals linked to solid measurements that directly support the goals and objectives of the overarching culture or enterprise.

Measuring the Right Things

One reason why cultures break down is that there is a disconnection between the purpose and vision of the organization and its purported goals, objectives and tactics. In strong, adaptive cultures, goals and objectives reflect the organization's purpose and vision, and cascade down from the top to every subculture and associate.

In an ideal culture, every individual would have specific, attainable goals linked to solid measurements that directly support the goals and objectives of the overarching culture or enterprise. Everyone would benefit from the nourishing relationship between his or her own goals and objectives and those of the organization. Each person could claim credit for his or her contribution to the organization's overall success. If individuals lack this empowering sense of contribution or don't feel that they share credit for the organization's success, you have to wonder what they are doing with their time.

In some cases, people perform tasks that bear little relationship to the organization's objectives. It's not surprising, therefore, that when companies go through a turnaround, they often find they can become leaner and still do better. These organizations discover that they are more productive as they focus more on urgent goals, and spend less on unnecessary tasks.

Choosing the Right Measurement Method

So how do you measure people? How do you come up with the right measurement criteria?

The fairest and most useful way is to look at and measure the behaviors and results that most benefit the goals and objectives of the organization. Take sales, for example. Do you measure salespeople by the total orders they take? Or do you measure the number of orders that actually result in deliveries and produce an acceptable level of profit for the organization?

An order by itself doesn't immediately produce a benefit that can be measured for the organization. Only when that order turns into a shipment, and the shipment results in income and profit to the company, is there a true benefit. In most cases it's far better to measure salespeople on net sales or gross profit than on gross orders.

In the same way, you don't measure the success of a manufacturing operation only by gross output. Instead, you measure the usable output that is free of defect. When you measure finance, you look at accounts receivables to see if they are being kept current and the proceeds made available to the enterprise. The amount of unpaid bills can be costly.

Almost everything can be measured. Granted, some things are harder to measure than others. An official with a large foundation told me how difficult it was to apply measurements to results in his field. The problem was that it took so long for the foundation to discern whether it was giving its money to the right recipients and whether those recipients were actually using their funding in productive ways and in keeping with the purpose of the foundation.

But even in situations where more judgment is required because of the lack of hard metrics, we can work with the people who are going to be measured to find those elements that are most meaningful to what the organization is trying to accomplish.

Perhaps in the case of a charity, a measurement can be taken of the number of constituents assisted in a certain period of time, or of how many new requests for services the charity received and how many were met.

Or consider bus drivers who drive the same route every day. One measurement of how well they serve their customers is how often they reach their stops on time. Another might be the number of compliments or complaints the bus company receives in a month's time. We can get a good picture of whether our treatment of customers is in line with our stated values by looking at the increase or decrease in complaints.

Similarly, airlines can measure how well they are serving their customers by checking their records for on-time arrivals, canceled flights and lost passenger luggage.

While nearly everything can be measured, the trick is to apply the right measurement method. It's a mistake to measure things over which the associate has little or no control. It's also a mistake to measure results that aren't significant to the goals and objectives of the organization.

The government has wrestled with setting measurements in its efforts to improve the effectiveness of its myriad operations. *The Primer on Performance Measurement* published by the Office of Management and Budget is a valuable resource that is available on the Internet (http://govinfo.library.unt.edu/npr/library/resource/gpraprmr.html). The primer defines four ways in which an objective can be measured. I have added efficiency and quality because they can also play important roles in establishing ways to measure performance.

1. *Input Measures* - Identify the AMOUNT OF RESOURCES needed to provide a particular product or service.
2. *Output Measures* - Represent the AMOUNT OF PRODUCTS OR SERVICES PROVIDED.
3. *Outcome Measures* - Assess the RESULTS OF A PROGRAM compared to its intended purpose.
4. *Impact Measures* - Assess the DIRECT OR INDIRECT EFFECTS that result from achieving the goals of a program.
5. *Efficiency Measures* - Also known as PRODUCTIVITY measures.
6. *Quality Measures* - Reflect the effectiveness in meeting the EXPECTATIONS OF CUSTOMERS AND STAKEHOLDERS.

The work by a number of government and private-sector organizations supports the belief that leaders and associates can identify objective ways to measure their own goals and those of the teams they are responsible for, as they seek to satisfy the needs, wants and values of both their internal and external customers.

Enlisting the Aid of Stakeholders

If you are struggling to find a way to measure a particular group's progress, a good solution is to bring together representatives of the group and a small number of its stakeholders.

After agreeing upon the purpose for the group you want to measure, you can then ask, "How do we get from here to there?" In other words, what would success look like if we fulfill our purpose? What are the measurable steps we have to take along the way?

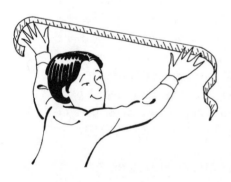

Stakeholders can provide new insight into measuring success

Your stakeholders can provide direct insight into how well the group, or an individual associate, is meeting the goals and objectives of the organization. Encouraging associates to explain the methodology for their assessment taps a new reservoir of information. Anyone who has a good understanding of a particular job's unique role in the organization is a source to help you determine valid measurements.

As a cultural tool, setting clear measurements communicates that we place a high value on the involvement of everyone in the organization.

Communicating measurements is a huge part of the culture at Springfield Remanufacturing, where each week leaders of the $33 million company "huddle" with associates and share all the figures that show how the company is faring. Associates use this information to adjust their own processes and performance to meet the organization's weekly, monthly or annual goals and objectives.

Involvement is one of the major corporate traits measured in the Denison Organizational Culture Survey. The survey measures the beliefs and assumptions employees have about their workplace.

I recall one outstanding example in the mid-1970s of how powerful associate involvement can be in setting measurable goals. At an annual sales meeting of the entire Marion Laboratories organization, founder Ewing Kauffman asked all his salespeople to discuss their performance goals with their spouses, who were also in attendance, and to print their commitments on the back of their business cards. While the salespeople were considering what to write, Mr. K talked about the results he might expect from some of the individuals in the audience and how proud he was of their past performance.

He then circulated among the sales representatives, collected their commitments and placed them in his coat pocket. Later, during meetings and in personal notes, he thanked associates who had made commitments to stretch their performance goals. It was amazing to hear how high the associates had set their goals, but more impressive to see how hard they worked to meet and even exceed them.

Such a level of commitment is consistent with great enterprises. They have passionate associates, who work together to set goals and measurements to reach their destination quickly, effectively and with great pride.

Going back to our space analogy, consider the crucial relationship and clear communication that was necessary between the scientists and engineers on the ground and the astronauts in space during that first journey to the moon. Each tense moment involved carefully calibrated measurements to ensure that there was enough fuel, that the systems on the shuttle were working properly and that the crew maintained its course.

Providing Timely Feedback

Associates of high-performance organizations want to monitor their performance and outcomes as much as, or more than, their supervisors do.

One of the key ways to encourage willing participation by associates in any measurement program is to allow them to select their own measurements. As a matter of fact, associates often set more stringent measurements for themselves than their manager is comfortable in setting for them.

But to sustain the success of a measurement program requires timely and positive feedback. Measurements without feedback tend to become meaningless, and after a while they atrophy and wither away. Associates can even come to resent them.

So the more timely the feedback, the more real it becomes. Feedback can be immediate, as it is in call centers where associates can often see on an electronic display how many customers are waiting and how long the average wait is. Feedback also can be in-depth, as when supervisors and associates pause periodically to reexamine their goals and objectives and compare them to current operating results. Whether done daily, weekly, monthly or quarterly, feedback allows leaders and associates to both adjust performance expectations and adapt to the changing needs of customers. Finally, feedback also serves to celebrate accomplishments.

Our "Marion-on-the-Move" outings at Marion Laboratories, in which we would all pile onto buses and head to the Kansas City Municipal Auditorium, were a form of positive feedback to the collective troops.

Marion's leaders shared with us the results for the period, what worked and what didn't, what we would focus on for the coming period and how that jelled with our long-term objectives.

Giving and receiving timely, objective feedback on performance expectations contributes to building a high-performance culture. While feedback is not necessarily linked with incentives, such as bonuses or salary increases, measurements are closely connected with a highly effective, performance-based recognition program.

Associates deserve timely feedback

How well associates accomplish their goals should be an integral part of any bonus plan. It should also be a basis for merit pay increases. Rewards for attaining goals that were mutually decided upon provide the incentive to embrace a system of measurements.

Matching rewards to measurements is the subject of Chapter 8.

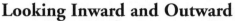

Looking Inward and Outward

While most organizations base their goals and measurements on past experience, many now use external benchmarking to compare themselves against the successful processes of other organizations.

What your organization does depends on your particular situation. If your business is unique, there may be few examples to compare against, so you are more likely to develop your own internal measurements. Still, much can be done by training associates to use measurement and feedback processes such as statistical process control to help them develop a sense of ownership of the processes they are responsible for using. Tools such as these can be successfully used whether you're focusing on what's happening on the plant floor or sales and marketing.

Almost anyone who can chart results can quickly begin to identify ways to improve his or her performance. And the majority of people derive satisfaction from seeing results go up.

Most people want to do as well as they can to develop goals and objectives that represent real accomplishment. America's productivity has increased markedly in the face of foreign competition over the last couple of decades. Some of these increases can be attributed to more organizations realizing the value of training associates to use tracking processes to measure their own effectiveness and the enterprise's overall performance.

It begins at the grassroots level with people setting their own goals, taking part in establishing measurements, having the necessary tools, knowledge and training to manage their jobs and getting positive feedback for their accomplishments.

In his book, *Measuring, Managing, and Maximizing Performance*, Will Kaydos does a beautiful job of looking at measurements from two perspectives. One is to create incentives to motivate people. The other is to provide information that can be used for comparison purposes by those whose work is being measured. Springfield Remanufacturing is an excellent example of leaders using measurements to create and communicate a feeling of involvement and desire for improved results at every level of the organization.

However, any performance method can be abused. Say you are measuring the number of ingots you pour each day in a steel plant. By not filling the molds all the way, or by using smaller molds, you can easily increase the number of ingots you make without increasing real production. So sheer numbers are not always the best measure.

In 1967, TWA had strong profits, and management executives were paid healthy bonuses. But the next year, actual profits fell. So the management extended the period of depreciation of its planes, thereby reducing its costs and making its profits appear greater than they actually were. But did the manipulation of measurements to produce an artificial increase in profits justify another round of bonuses? Probably not.

The point is that leaders need to be aware of the frailties inherent in measurement methodologies and act accordingly.

Focusing on Customer Needs

The closer a job gets to the output of the organization, the easier it is to measure.

That's why sales jobs are relatively easy to measure and lend themselves to effective rewards programs. But Kaydos makes a strong case that any meaningful job has output that can be measured. He points out that 80 percent of an organization's costs are for white-collar jobs. And yet, we only measure performances of 5 percent of the white-collar jobs. He contends that while it may be more difficult to develop measurements for white-collar positions, some unit of output can be found and measured for essentially any position.

> *The closer a job gets to the output of the organization, the easier it is to measure.*

One thing that can be measured is customer satisfaction. Customers make decisions either to buy and become long-term customers or to reject a company and its products, based upon their satisfaction with the product and the service.

This also includes satisfying our internal customers. As the head of marketing at Marion Laboratories, I went to many product review meetings, where various product groups would make their pitches to the sales leadership. Usually, you could quickly tell when one product group was on track and another was not.

The difference in every case was that the on-track product group did a better job of identifying with the needs of the sales department and its external customers. The sample materials produced by the groups that excelled demonstrated what they had learned from their internal customers. The product groups that didn't measure up, on the other hand, not only produced poorer quality materials, it was clear they hadn't properly engaged their internal customers—the sales staff—in the development and planning of their programs.

Measuring different departments through the eyes of both their internal stakeholders and their external customers can be revealing. Focusing on how well their organizations are satisfying customers' needs can help leaders determine the direction they want the enterprise to go, structure the processes that support the organization and develop useful measurements that motivate associates to meet its goals and objectives.

Clearly, measurements play a pivotal role in building a successful organization. Fitting the measurements piece into our cube moves us closer to the objectives of cultural renewal: improving the bottom line, attracting, motivating and retaining talent, and adapting to change.

Cultural Conscience Checklist	Yes	No
• Are you measuring the right things?		
• Are associates involved in setting their own goals and measurements?		
• Do the associates of your organization receive timely feedback on their progress?		
• Do your measurement methods empower associates to improve their processes and outcomes?		

CHAPTER 8

Rewards: More Than Money

"While money is important to employees, what tends to motivate them to perform—and to perform at higher levels—is the thoughtful, personal kind of recognition that signifies true appreciation for a job well done."

—Bob Nelson
Author, *1001 Ways to Reward Employees*[28]

Rewards Defined:

The processes utilized to recognize associates for their behaviors and contributions to the organization.

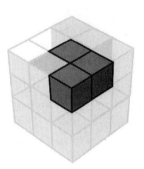

The Process:

- Continuously assess and revise extrinsic rewards (monetary) to ensure they are effectively rewarding associates for desired behaviors and outcomes
- Diligently use intrinsic rewards (non-monetary) to effectively recognize individuals and teams for excellence and accomplishment of challenging objectives

As mentioned in Chapter 3, one of the core values at Marion Laboratories simply read: "Those who produce should share in the results."

This phrase sums up the guiding philosophy of one of the most motivating cultures in American business—before it was absorbed into a succession of organizations that were less passionate about sustaining its highly productive workplace culture.

Ewing Kauffman, the legendary president of Marion, shared the results very, very well with his associates. More than 600 became millionaires. Many people mistakenly attribute adherence to that value only to Mr. Kauffman's altruism. Mr. K was also a gambler. And he gambled on what he knew about human nature. He was persuaded there was a better way to link Marion's results with profits by creating strong compensation incentives that boosted the rewards and thus the productivity of his associates.

A traditional approach that links production to profits usually goes like this: If the organization accomplishes its objectives, here is what we'll make in profit. But what if you provided greater incentives that encouraged your associates to create a larger margin of profit? Wouldn't you be happy to share more of your success with them? Of course, you would.

That's just what Mr. K and the executives of Marion Labs did. They devised a compensation and benefit package that linked rewards to objectives that produced more profit. And it worked. Mr. K realized early on that if you can involve your employees in making the organization more successful through effective compensation and rewards processes, they push harder for success, and make it pay—for the company and for themselves.

The more profit the company made, the more was shared with the associates. With this added incentive, the associates saw they had a very real financial and cultural stake in improving the bottom line.

Consider, for instance, my division, Marion Health and Safety. When I joined the company we were compensating our sales force based on gross sales. The incentive was to go out and sell all you could, at whatever price you could get your sales manager to approve, because that way you could sell more units, right? The problem with that logic, though, is that even if you increased your sales, it didn't mean you increased your profits.

So we changed the bonus and compensation plan and linked it to gross profits instead of gross sales. The more profit each salesperson generated, the more money the company made. The more money Marion made, the more the salespeople made in increased compensation and bonuses. Every division of Marion had highly motivated salespeople due to the emphasis placed on making sure that the compensation met the needs of the salesperson, the company and even the customer. When Marion Laboratories was sold to Dow Chemical in 1989, it had the highest levels of sales and profits per associate in the pharmaceutical industry, not a small claim considering that the pharmaceutical industry is already noted for being one of the highest profit industry categories globally.

Appropriate rewards, delivered in a timely manner, can enforce desired behavior, encourage a positive output and raise employee morale. Rewards help people focus on what it takes to achieve the goals and objectives set for the enterprise and for its subcultures.

> *Rewards give meaning to the measurements put in place to help the organization reach its goals and objectives.*

An effective system of rewards is the last crucial element that completes our cultural cube. Rewards give meaning to the measurements put in place to help the organization reach its goals and objectives. But often, the process of providing rewards is misguided, taken for granted or performed so haphazardly that it loses much of its original meaning and purpose.

That's why it is imperative for cultural leaders to enforce the use of rewards by consistently monitoring how they are administered and ensuring that they achieve their intended purpose.

It's also instructive to understand how to balance different types of rewards, as people respond to the same recognition differently. No one reward motivates everyone. And using the same reward—the traditional Employee of the Month Award—year after year grows stale, eventually eliciting little more than a shrug from associates.

The reward should match the personality and the job of the individual, as well as be competitive with industry standards. Some employees prefer to see their names highlighted in the company newsletter. Others would rather be recognized with cash. Some simply want a commission and bonus plan that recognizes their ability to push ahead of everyone else. The key is to find and maintain the right balance that works for you and your organization. Specific rewards can be so overused that instead of being an incentive, they become a routine perk of the job. A Christmas turkey that is given to everyone after a particularly great year, and is then given out to everyone each year thereafter, quickly becomes an expected tradition rather than a reward for a job well done. In several cases the "Christmas turkey" has wound up in the union contract.

Regardless of the system you choose, rewards should be timely and should clearly convey that you value a person's achievements. If you don't know what revs up one of your associates—ask! You'll get your answer. And every individual will think more of you for asking.

Extrinsic and Intrinsic Rewards

There are two kinds of rewards: extrinsic and intrinsic. Extrinsic rewards involve rewarding employees with financial incentives, such as salaries, bonus plans, profit sharing and paid health benefits. Intrinsic rewards are primarily non-financial, and are intended to formally or informally recognize a person's inner drive toward self-fulfillment, acceptance and success. Intrinsic rewards might include a gift certificate to a health spa, a day off or a letter of recognition from the boss.

Extrinsic Rewards	Intrinsic Rewards
Salary	Formal Recognition
Bonus	Informal Recognition
Fringe Benefits	Peer Recognition
Retirement Funding	Involvement
Profit Sharing	Empowerment

Reward types

Whatever the rewards, leaders get more mileage out of them by keeping them fresh, motivating and adaptable to market and organizational changes. Rewards should stay current with the organization's objectives, for instance, anticipating product life-cycle changes.

While money remains an important incentive, studies have found that when employees are surveyed about why they leave a job, they often list a lack of recognition by their bosses and limited advancement opportunities ahead of how they feel about their incomes.

When we assume that monetary rewards are the most important human driver, we overlook basic psychology. Individuals are not motivated by money to the same degree. If you are having trouble making the house payment,

Money is never the whole answer

money can be extremely important. But if you are comfortable with your economic status, money becomes less of an incentive for greater performance.

The key to building effective cultures is rooted in human behavior. We have a range of needs, best expressed in Abraham Maslow's hierarchy of human needs.[29] At the base of his pyramid is the need for physical comfort. As physical comforts are satisfied, our needs become more emotional and linked to the psyche, so that they influence our self-esteem, self-worth and self-fulfillment.

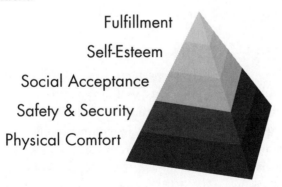

Fulfillment

Self-Esteem

Social Acceptance

Safety & Security

Physical Comfort

Maslow's hierarchy of human needs

115

Maslow believed that all of us strive to be accepted by others and to reach a point where we are happy with ourselves. Ultimately, the goal is to reach an inner sense of fulfillment that transcends physical comforts. People work their way through this passage of needs at different times in their lives and at a different pace.

As a result, everyone has separate needs at different levels, depending on personality and current circumstances. So if you are developing a compensation plan that depends only upon the use of money to motivate everyone, it is ill conceived from the outset and will fail, or at least fail to optimize the potential of your organization.

We must satisfy our basic needs. Most of us can't live without money, for example. And it's true that some people aspire to jobs that carry very high salaries. But others are content to take jobs that will never make them rich. They may not have the drive to achieve a higher-paying job, or they may enjoy their current job, career choice or lifestyle so much that they are unwilling to give it up for a job that pays better.

How does this apply to your organization? Your basic extrinsic rewards programs must meet the needs of the people you want to attract to the enterprise. The culture must then reward them with a fair compensation plan. But even after you build an effective, incentive-based compensation plan, you are only part of the way to a balanced rewards system.

By understanding basic human psychology, you can create a rewards system that addresses all levels of your employees' needs. An ideal program would satisfy basic needs, include a compensation-incentive program but also nurture the kind of recognition that helps an associate answer the important question: "What's really important in my life? What do I really want to accomplish?"—the highest level of Maslow's pyramid.

Finding the Right Balance

Tom McCoy's 1992 book *Compensation and Motivation* does an excellent job of exploring the potential of well-designed compensation plans that incorporate both extrinsic and intrinsic rewards. McCoy has become one of the biggest proponents of a rewards system that recognizes people for positive behaviors and productive output tied to measurement processes that are also appropriately designed and implemented. He thinks that a Behavior-Based Incentive Compensation (BBIC) system can dramatically improve performance and culture by linking compensation and performance.

I believe with McCoy that we underutilize incentive-based compensation plans that involve using extrinsic rewards to improve output. Twenty years ago such programs were seldom used, especially in white-collar environments. Now, at least 50 percent of associates are in some form of incentive-based compensation plan. Indeed, as we saw in Chapter 7, every job has some measurable output. And if you can measure the output, some portion of that person's compensation ought to be made attributable to his or her real output.

Another way to approach incentive-based compensation is to create a bonus pool. This way, when executives are highly compensated because of the organization's top-flight performance, the money in the bonus pool is shared, at some level, with all associates, commensurate with their contributions to the success of the organization's goals and objectives.

Cultural leaders can incorporate McCoy's BBIC system by:
- Identifying their organization's needs
- Establishing clear objectives for each part of the organization
- Developing objective measurement methods for each of the key objectives
- Choosing the right behavioral and compensation approach to address those needs
- Combining these elements in an incentive-based compensation program that promotes top performance and the best return

McCoy suggests that as leaders seek to strike a balance that is good for the organization, the customers and the employees, they face three choices for lining up compensation plans with organizational objectives:

1. Match compensation with the level of performance; don't overpay for the results being achieved.
2. Maintain current levels of compensation but increase the levels of performance by using intrinsic rewards that help to mold the desired behavior leading to improved results.
3. Adopt a system that makes compensation contingent upon specific performance; build an incentive-based plan that progressively pays more as behavior changes and results improve.[30]

Implicit in these choices is McCoy's caution that in many cases we go overboard trying to create elaborate incentive-based compensation plans while overlooking the equally powerful opportunities offered by intrinsic rewards. The best approach is a mix of both kinds of rewards.

The results sought are what you as the leader and the associates involved are expecting a particular unit or an individual to produce—the goals and objectives that have been agreed upon. Measurements reflect how well the employee did in meeting these goals and objectives, and the rewards are the recognition for achieving or exceeding them. If the goals are not met, the leader and the associate or workgroup need to determine the reasons for failing to reach the objective or whether the objective was even appropriate. Then they need to decide what the goals, measurements and rewards should be.

This focus on behavior occurs around a shared belief system and a team of people with common goals and objectives, who weave together complementary but different job skills and talents. The message is communicated to associates: "We want to become more innovative; help us to innovate, thereby improving results and we will reward you and others who work together."

An Incentive-Based Compensation Story

A couple of years ago, when I was preparing to retire from corporate life, I unexpectedly experienced an example of how extrinsic rewards can effectively focus associates' efforts and encourage a desired behavior.

Before leaving a previous employer, I had contacted my financial advisor, Max Greer. My wife and I had been investing through my employer's benefits program and now I wanted some advice on what to do with my investments upon retirement.

When I phoned Max, I expected the person who answered my call to be polite. But I hadn't expected that she would be so attentive to our needs and so considerate of my time as was the case. Carol Sloan, the receptionist among other duties, treated me like an old friend whom she was very happy to hear from.

After saying hello, I mentioned I would like to schedule an appointment with Max to review my portfolio. That was Carol's cue to give me the full, red-carpet treatment.

"Mr. Haney, I'm so happy we'll be working with you again," Carol said, practically beaming over the telephone. She was pleased to make an appointment for my wife and me, "I can't wait to see you and Julia again," she said, concluding the conversation.

When we arrived for the appointment, I told Max about my conversation with Carol and how impressed I was by the warm reception and the attitude of "ownership" she displayed each time I talked to her.

Now everyone, from administrative support staff to financial advisors, shared in the rewards of the firm's profits. So, when the business grew, so did everybody's paycheck.

Max was not surprised one bit. Since we had last talked, he had restructured some of the functions at the firm, including the compensation plan. Now everyone, from administrative support staff to financial advisors, shared in the rewards of the firm's profits. So, when the business grew, so did everybody's paycheck.

Not only that, Max had flattened the company's organizational structure, with the result that everyone had a say in what went on, including the compensation plan and even who got hired. Job descriptions had grown broader and more diverse as the staff willingly took on more responsibilities. People responded like a close-knit team, taking responsibility for the firm's successes, and setbacks.

As a client, I was comfortable that our investments were in excellent hands and I felt secure knowing that everyone in Max's organization had a stake in helping us nurture our retirement nest egg.

My observations and discussions with Max and numerous other managers who are effectively using incentive-based compensation programs have reinforced my strong belief that incentive-based compensation is too often overlooked as a powerful driver of performance at every level of organizations.

You Have Control over Intrinsic Rewards

Face it. In many cases subcultural leaders have little if any control over the extrinsic rewards of the enterprise as they are tied to the organization-wide budgets and compensation plans. But that should not be seen as a barrier for you to improve the overall rewards processes in your area of responsibility. Money is not the cure-all for your rewards processes anyway.

While you may have little control over the extrinsic rewards, you do have almost total control over the use of intrinsic (non-cash) rewards. That said, I hasten to add that most managers could do a better job of formally or informally recognizing people for their contributions to the organization. How often do you pass a note of thanks to an associate, for example?

When I ask an audience at one of my workshops, "Are you doing a good job of implementing intrinsic rewards?," almost without exception, everybody sheepishly responds, "No, I never do enough."

Extrinsic rewards are only half of the reason why your employees stick with you—or look for a new job somewhere else. Hopefully, what entices them to stay, in large measure, is their sense of belonging and pride, precipitated by the recognition they receive from their peers, their leaders and their customers for a job well done.

This is why leaders can't let recognition wane. They can't afford to become so busy solving problems, fixing processes, hiring, firing and focusing on the bureaucracy that they fail to recognize their associates. Making the recognition of associates a habit ensures it stays on your daily to-do list.

That is why Bob Nelson's book, *1001 Ways to Reward Employees*, is such a gift. You can't go five pages into the book without saying, "Oh my gosh, this is so easy." But why do we need somebody to beat us over the head and show us the importance of giving recognition to associates for their positive contributions?

It makes so much sense to shape behavior by recognizing someone for doing good work, catching people at it when they least expect, giving them more responsibility and then recognizing them for their growing list of successes. Suggestions for intrinsic rewards abound: tickets to a football game, an improved office location, time off, a certificate for a back massage, public praise at an office meeting, a simple thank-you. The list becomes endless, when you care to think about it.

Leaders have a great deal of control over providing intrinsic rewards, allowing them to mine rewards as a natural resource to dramatically improve their workplace culture. People need and want motivation in their lives. But their needs are different, as discussed earlier.

Intrinsic rewards are always cited as the force for motivating employees of the 100 companies on *Fortune* magazine's annual "100 Best Companies to Work for in America" list. In conjunction with *Fortune's* research, the Gallup Organization polled 55,000 workers in a 1998 survey of the relationship between employee attitudes and company performance. Pollsters found that four attitudes correlate with higher profits:

Spontaneous informal recognition pays big dividends

"Workers feel they are given the opportunity to do what they do best every day; they believe their opinions count; they sense that their fellow workers are committed to quality; and they've made a direct connection between their work and the company's mission. These echo loudly the comments we heard over and over from employees at companies on the 100 Best list."[31]

And as with the other five elements of culture, recognizing employees pays—by creating an environment where motivated employees take pride in and ownership of the organization's success. In a 1998 Ernst & Young report,[32] researchers found that large investors tend to buy stock in companies that can attract and retain talented individuals.

Some companies have become famous for using a combination of extrinsic and intrinsic rewards. For example, top officials at Mary Kay Cosmetics discovered early on that people strive to succeed for their own self-esteem and self-fulfillment as much as for financial rewards.

As a result, Mary Kay business meetings are joyous celebrations. Top salespeople are not only rewarded with strong compensation and the ubiquitous pink Cadillac, they are also cheered by their peers and praised by the leaders of the company as if they'd won the lottery.

In my own career, I have seen employee motivation lead to some incredible results. Low unemployment and a relatively strong economy make this a prime time for taking a good look at how well you recognize and reward your associates, and what you do to attract and keep top talent.

The skilled labor pool is shrinking. And loyalty to organizations among many young people is short-lived. These new workers are constantly on the lookout for new opportunities, greater financial remuneration and workplaces that fit their lifestyles.

Effective rewards systems are necessary to match the needs of this new generation of employees. Organizations need committed and knowledgeable associates if they want to build cultures that are nimble enough to adapt to the rapid changes that buffet their industries today. Old-style, hierarchical organizations that tell employees what to think, what to do and when to do it are dying.

Leaders who support cultures that can inspire their associates to care about the purpose and vision of the organization and to cater to the changing needs, wants and values of their customers can draw strength from surveys that show employees are very satisfied with work cultures that believe in well-conceived and well-implemented goal setting, measurements and recognition plans. And we know that performance measurements, when reinforced with appropriate rewards processes, result in successes that extend directly to the bottom line.

Cultural Conscience Checklist	Yes	No
• Are extrinsic rewards tied to the performance of each associate in your organization?		
• Do employees relate their compensation to the results they achieve for the organization?		
• Are associates regularly given opportunities to gain recognition and other intrinsic rewards?		
• Is there a formal process in place to recognize outstanding performance by teams and/or individuals?		
• Are leaders timely with their informal recognition of associates?		

CHAPTER 9

Putting the Cube Back Together: Making Your Culture Pay

"Culture is deep, extensive, and stable. It cannot be taken lightly. If you do not manage culture, it manages you, and you may not even be aware of the extent to which this is happening."

—Edgar H. Schein
Author, *The Corporate Culture Survival Guide* [33]

At this point you may be thinking, "You make many really good points, but how do I tackle the process of using these thoughts in optimizing my own organizational culture? What are the steps that my leadership team and I should take first?" Stated differently, "How do I make the most out of my cultural cube?"

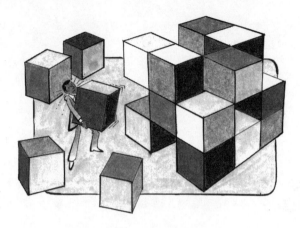

Build culture one block at a time

The answer is, you build the cube one step at a time. The building or rebuilding process begins with some very critical, specific steps I like to refer to as the "cultural renewal process."

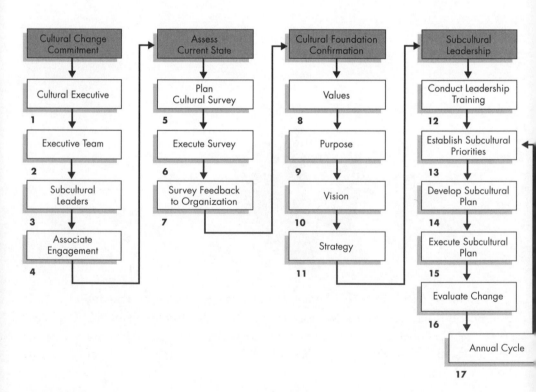

The cultural renewal process

This flowchart depicts the steps to dramatically improving cultural effectiveness. While one might be tempted to take a shortcut, the reality is there are no quick and easy ways to building a highly effective culture. Still, what might first appear like many time-consuming steps will soon become a logical process that, when carefully followed, actually reduces the time required to maximize cultural effectiveness.

Gaining Commitment

Whether you are trying to change the culture of the entire enterprise or of a single subculture, gaining commitment from the top leaders is the first order of business.

1. *Cultural Executive Commitment*

"Cultural executive commitment" means the total commitment of your organization's "head"—be it the CEO or maybe yourself as the head of the subculture—to undertaking the cultural renewal process. This commitment stems from a basic understanding of what workplace culture is and the critical elements affecting it.

In addition, it reflects a deep desire to lead that culture to excellence, and to build an organization blessed with associates who are driven to make their workplace and themselves successful. The "committed executive" understands the importance of engaging the other leaders in this exciting journey, a journey without end, to organizational excellence.

The term "cultural executive commitment" is very carefully chosen. While most of us have been told that cultural change must begin with the CEO or the chairman of the board, I have found that change can begin anywhere in an organization, at any leadership level. Every organizational leader needs to understand and willingly accept his or her role—and responsibility—as a cultural leader of the organization.

This chapter, like the rest of this book, is written for emerging leaders at any level of the organization who are motivated to build or rebuild an effective workplace culture. If you aren't the top leader of the enterprise, you still have a responsibility to do everything possible to improve your own organizational subculture.

Cultural Change
Commitment

↓

Cultural Executive

1 ↓

Executive Team

2 ↓

Subcultural
Leaders

3 ↓

Associate
Engagement

4

While it may be ideal for cultural renewal to start at the very top, there are many potential options and resources available to you and your organization within the context of your own area of responsibility. If there are limitations on the amount of initiative you can take, acknowledge them and dedicate yourself to improving your organization, using the tools within your control and the latitude you do have.

2. *Executive Team Commitment*

The cultural executives at every level of your organization can be helped to understand their responsibility for cultural renewal within their respective areas. If these executives report to you, nurture their enthusiasm and support for the process. Everyone on your executive team needs to become comfortable with the cultural model, the rationale for cultural change, and the process proposed for his or her area of responsibility in the organization. The initial executive cultural engagement sessions should generally last about three hours and answer the following questions:

- What is organizational culture?
- What makes a culture effective?
- Do great cultures produce better results?
- Why do we need to improve our culture?
- What will my role be in the process?
- What are the critical elements of culture?
- How do we determine the strengths and weaknesses of our present culture?
- What are the specific process steps for improving our culture?

I have found that this orientation excites most leaders to improve the culture of their own area of responsibility while working to develop the culture of the entire enterprise as well. When they begin to understand the process and are convinced of the executive team's commitment, the remaining leaders tend to become true supporters and active participants. Now, you may not convince every single leader of this undertaking's importance at first, but most readily become very committed to the process. It's desirable but not essential that the entire executive team buys into the cultural renewal process. In every cultural enhancement process there will be early adopters, laggards and occasionally a manager who just isn't into it or isn't capable of this type of leadership.

Enterprise-wide cultures are actually changed by the division and department leaders, or subcultural leaders, not by the single top executive of the organization. Long ago I realized that there are always different levels of acceptance and commitment to cultural change initiatives. Even so, you can develop a dynamic group of people who buy into and have a deep appreciation for the process of cultural renewal.

When I was beginning my consulting practice, I worked with a large health care system that decided to use the executive team orientation as a pilot project. I conducted the orientation meeting with executives from four of the system's hospitals and one of its smaller for-profit ventures. At this meeting, we planned on signing up one of the four hospital teams and a smaller for-profit venture for the organization's initial cultural renewal process. As it turned out, all four of the hospital executive teams insisted on being included.

At the end of the executive team orientation, a go or no-go decision needs to be made. If the "committed executive" and the newly "committed executive team" are ready to move forward, the next step is a logical one—ensuring the engagement of the subcultural leaders.

3. *Subcultural Leadership Engagement*

Once senior leaders are committed, the next step is engaging the directors, managers, and supervisors. The best way to do that is through a motivational meeting conducted by the senior executive and several executive team members, in some cases supported by an outside consultant or facilitator. A key objective of this meeting is to secure the wholehearted support of the subcultural leaders.

Points to cover in this leadership engagement meeting include:
- A definition of "organizational culture"
- The benefits of great cultures
- The critical elements of culture

- The kind of culture we want in our organization
- How we will assess our culture today
- Understanding the steps of cultural renewal
- Understanding their roles as subcultural leaders

These meetings can result in energetic support when the presenting leaders demonstrate their own commitment. First-line managers and supervisors are usually very eager to become involved in the renewal process because they often recognize the need to pay more attention to culture and are encouraged by their leaders' new-found knowledge and commitment to cultural enhancement.

4. *Associate Engagement*

Effective cultural leaders understand the need to engage every leader and every associate in the renewal process. When they are made a part of the process, associates at every level in most cases genuinely welcome, rather than resist, your efforts, as long as you are sincere. You can demonstrate your sincerity with behavior that is consistent with what you are asking them to do—by walking the talk.

I have found that the best time to conduct the associate engagement session is just prior to asking the associates to complete a formal cultural survey such as the Denison Organizational Culture Survey, if it is to be used as a part of your renewal process. If a formal cultural survey is not part of your planned approach, it remains important to engage your associates through some other means that defines and validates their roles.

The top executive of the organization and one or more members of the executive team should conduct this associate engagement session. The presentation should be brief (no longer than one hour) and should answer the following questions for associates:

- What is organizational culture?
- What are the critical elements of culture?
- What makes a culture really effective?
- Why do we want to improve our culture?
- How will we determine our current cultural needs?

- What's our process for cultural improvement?
- What's my role in the process?
- What's in it for me?

Assessing the Current State

A necessary step in any cultural renewal process is taking time to assess the strengths and weaknesses of the current culture and its subcultures.

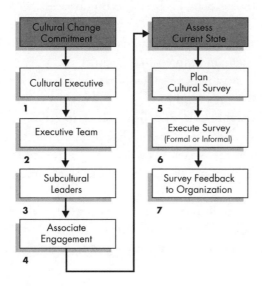

5. *Plan Cultural Survey*

Understanding where your organization is today is critically important to the cultural renewal process. There are several ways to go about making this assessment. Here we will look at three: informal cultural assessment, formal cultural survey and a tool we have developed called "Cultural Conscience."

Informal Cultural Assessment. An informal appraisal can involve leaders at every level addressing questions, much like those presented in the Cultural Conscience Checklist at the end of each of the chapters in this book. You can expand upon these questions to reflect your organization's unique characteristics.

Leaders going through this process for the first time often have an inflated view of their culture. For that reason, presenting a series of probing questions on a survey form that are then responded to by all associates can provide a more objective and immediate assessment of a culture and enable leaders to set more appropriate priorities.

Formal Cultural Survey. A formal cultural assessment provides a broad sampling of all associates at every level of the organization. While a formal survey involves some expense, it has offsetting benefits, which include:

- The ability to assess the overall culture and the subcultures in a consistent and professional manner
- Objective measurement and comparison to similar cultures outside your organization
- Establishment of a baseline from which to begin
- The ability to establish appropriate priorities for change
- Buy-in from the associates because they are asked to share their thoughts about the culture of the organization

A number of cultural survey instruments are available. As mentioned, I have had success using the Denison Organizational Culture Survey. This survey links organizational culture to tangible bottom-line performance measures such as:

- Profitability
- Innovation
- Sales growth
- Market share
- Quality
- Employee satisfaction

For more than 20 years, Dr. Daniel Denison of the University of Michigan Business School has studied high- and low-performing organizations' cultures. Based on this research, he found that the following four traits have a significant impact on organizational performance:

- *Involvement:* Building human capability, ownership, and responsibility
- *Consistency:* Defining the values and the organization's systems that are the basis of a strong culture
- *Adaptability:* Translating the demands of the business environment into action
- *Mission:* Defining a meaningful long-term direction for the organization

Usually, it is difficult to link survey results to the business itself. However, the Denison survey translates complex behavioral concepts into tangible everyday business actions and strategies, and compares your culture's capacity to produce results with over 450 other organizational cultures.

This allows you to discern and develop priorities for cultural revitalization that are unique to your culture and its subcultures. Consequently, it enables leaders, stakeholders and associates at all levels to understand the impact their culture has on the organization's performance. They can then redirect their culture to take advantage of strengths and minimize weaknesses.

Cultural Conscience Tool. The Visionomics Cultural Conscience tool is a software-based assessment program designed to complement the cultural renewal process.[34] Managers can use this tool in developing and renewing cultural enhancement initiatives. The program generates questions to help leaders evaluate each of the cultural elements within the context of their own organization or department. It also suggests initiatives they can incorporate into their annual planning processes, resulting in goals and objectives that relate directly to cultural improvement.

6. *Execute Survey (Formal Survey)*

The best way to execute a formal cultural survey such as the Denison Organizational Culture Survey is for each leader to administer the survey to his or her employees at one sitting over coffee or during a team meeting. This ensures that each employee completes the survey and thereby contributes to its validity.

Individual surveys are typically assigned a "litho number" so each respondent can be identified with the appropriate subculture. The number should be explained when the surveys are handed out to assure associates that their anonymity is protected. Completed surveys are returned to a common box, again to protect anonymity, and sent to a scoring center for processing. This process takes about ten days.

Some of the most successful change processes I have been involved with used the survey session as a way to engage and inform associates about the cultural renewal process.

7. *Survey Feedback to Organization*

Results of individual surveys are combined at the scoring center to create both graphic and narrative information, profiling your organization and each of its subcultures.

As part of the process your organization is compared with more than 450 organizations representing more than 50,000 employees who have also been surveyed. This comparison is graphically presented in an illustration, called a circumplex, which contrasts the strengths and weaknesses of your organization's culture and subcultures, based on the current beliefs and assumptions your associates have about those cultures.

The Denison Organizational Culture Survey reports beliefs and assumptions that employees have about the organization's cultural traits that most impact performance: involvement, consistency, adaptability, and mission. The results are presented in percentile gradients of 25th, 50th, 75th and 100th, so leaders can easily assess their employees' beliefs and assumptions, compare them with those of other organizations and determine the direction and priorities for needed changes. The survey report provides line-by-line detail on how each question was answered by your associates and points out trends and areas of concern, opportunity or praise. As an example, if an enterprise or subculture scored low on awareness of core values or reported that the leaders fail to live up to the values, that calls attention to a very good place to begin the cultural renewal process.

Once the reports are in, it is helpful to hold feedback meetings before launching the cultural renewal process. Here employees should be able to openly discuss their beliefs and assumptions about their culture.

Feedback sessions can turn into "engagement parties" that encourage leaders and associates alike to get excited about the prospects for change and

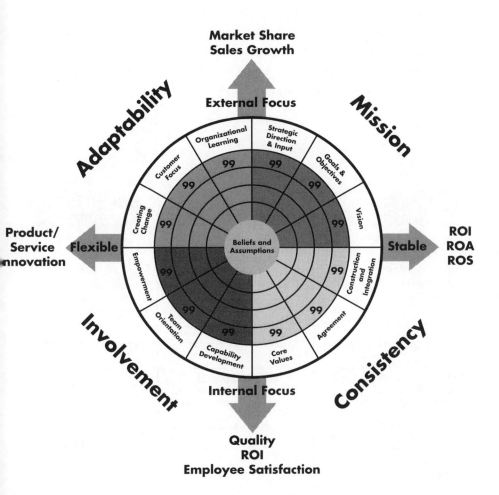

Denison cultural survey circumplex

their roles in bringing it about. Sessions can be used for brainstorming about the issues and opportunities facing the organization, leading to a head start on the renewal process.

Conducting additional surveys periodically provides objective measurements of the organization's progress toward achieving a high-performance culture.

Establishing a Cultural Foundation

Establishing a cultural foundation is an important step in creating a basis for cultural and subcultural leadership, and for long-term planning. It begins the process of building a structure that allows leaders to consistently communicate the direction they want to take the organization and measure the organization's progress towards its vision.

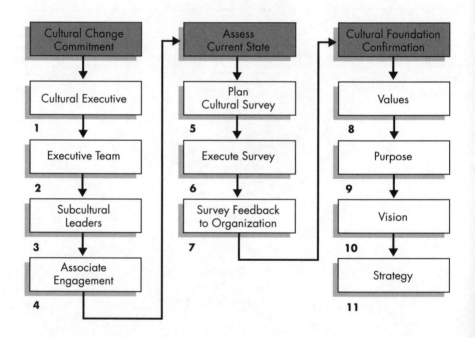

8. *Values*

In the most effective organizational cultures, top leaders willingly take responsibility for ensuring the development of core values.

When the overarching culture lacks a clear set of core values, it falls to the subcultural leaders to encourage the organizational leaders above them to develop core values for the entire enterprise. If that is not practical, subcultural leaders should seek to establish four to six core values that guide their own department or division.

Core values lay the foundation for cultural change. So it is vital that every cultural leader has in place a meaningful set of core values. The process for determining core values outlined in Chapter 3 can be effectively used as a springboard for cultural renewal.

9. *Purpose*

While the purpose (your organization's reason for being) of the total enterprise may be crystal clear to the leaders, it is still necessary to clarify that purpose for all associates so that they understand the organization's reason for being. Having an organizational purpose that is shared by every organizational unit (subculture) provides the necessary basis for creating vision, strategies, tactics, goals and objectives. It also helps determine the best ways to measure and reward team and individual performance.

10. *Vision*

Organizational vision (your future state) provides the associates with a common understanding and a clearer picture of the organization's future appearance.

Properly conceived, communicated and institutionalized, the vision for the organization or subculture should inspire and create enthusiasm for reaching a desirable future state.

11. *Strategy*

Subcultural leaders take their cue for determining and planning the tactical steps their departments will execute from the overarching strategic goals set for the enterprise by its top leaders. Clear strategic direction from above is necessary, then, to ensure that subcultures develop their own supporting strategies.

Conducting Subcultural Leadership Training

Training subcultural leaders gives them the knowledge and tools required to initiate and sustain the cultural renewal process.

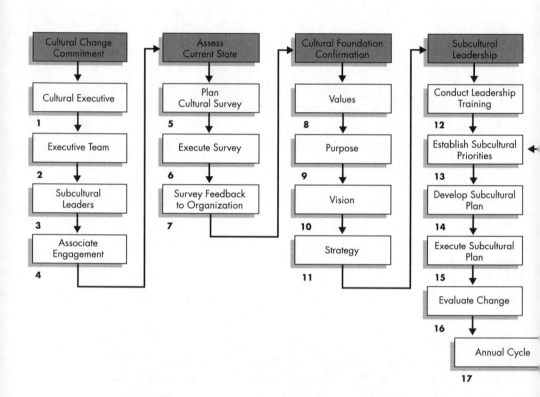

12. Conduct Leadership Training

Individual leaders at all levels share the responsibility for developing a strong and adaptive culture. They demonstrate this responsibility by working with their teams on a daily basis to make sure every associate has specific operating and cultural goals, and that these goals exist in concert with the purpose, vision and strategies of the organization. Very little change can be made in any culture until these subcultural leaders:

- Have a consistent understanding of organizational culture
- Enthusiastically assume a strong role in the cultural renewal process
- Are excited about and committed to the change process
- Understand where their culture is today
- Possess the skills necessary to lead cultural change
- Develop an effective plan for cultural change in their organization

Leaders trained to understand the vital role of culture in the life of the organization become well-rounded individuals who enthusiastically promote and enforce positive values and behaviors among their associates.

Cultural leadership training should go beyond the traditional management skills of interviewing, coaching and counseling. Leaders trained to understand the vital role of culture in the life of the organization become well-rounded individuals who enthusiastically promote and enforce positive values and behaviors among their associates. These leaders know that strong, adaptive cultures don't happen by chance, and they become missionaries who want to spread the word throughout the enterprise.

The areas of emphasis for specific cultural leadership training should include:

1. Understanding Cultural Leadership
    - The importance of cultural effectiveness
    - The critical elements of strong, adaptive cultures
    - The art and science of communicating the cultural change process
    - The ability to overcome objections to cultural change

2. Personalities and Change
- Defining the characteristics of a cultural leader
- Understanding one's own personality (utilizing a simple but objective personality assessment tool)
- Understanding the dynamics of other personality styles
- Dealing effectively with other personality styles during the change process

   3. Setting and Managing Cultural Priorities
- Establishing cultural priorities (using formal and/or informal methods)
- Establishing strategies, tactics, and goals and objectives for change
- Coaching and counseling
- Tracking, measuring and reporting
- Planning and integrating annual cultural change initiatives

Leaders in the organization who have already gone through a training process can train subcultural leaders. Professional trainers and consultants may also be hired to coordinate the early steps in the cultural renewal process.

13. *Establish Subcultural Priorities*

After their training, your organization's leaders should be ready to analyze the feedback from the associate surveys and the individual appraisals of the strengths and weaknesses of their present cultures. Mining the survey data will bring to light new resources and knowledge that will help in developing the plan for cultural renewal, set priorities and engage the participation of the associates at every cultural level.

All of the organization's leaders should be working closely together at this phase in the cultural renewal planning process, especially in establishing the organization's crucial core values. It is best to start by developing an overall plan at the top of the enterprise that includes: core values, purpose, vision and strategic intent. With these critical components in place, the subcultural leaders are much better prepared to develop their own subcultural components that directly complement those of the overarching culture or enterprise.

At the same time, subcultural leaders may discover that their own departments have unique priorities that do not require coordination with other departments. For example, a set of clear core values may be integrated well into some of the enterprise's subcultures but not as well into others. Leaders should make it a priority to communicate, reinforce and enforce the overall core values of the organization in such a way that they become models that can be readily followed by each of the organization's subcultures.

If your organization does not have a set of core values or is not adhering to established ones, start there. Beyond values, an objective appraisal of any organization, and any level of the organization, will uncover significant opportunities for cultural enhancement. Comparing the strengths of your present culture with the six elements that make up the Visionomics Cube should prompt a number of hard questions. By asking and answering these questions, a list of issues and opportunities can be developed and refined into a set of meaningful cultural priorities.

Always keep in mind that cultural change is a long and eventful journey of discovery. Some leaders are tempted to place microscopic attention on each weakness they find, but this is a mistake that wastes time and energy. Set your sights high and pick your priorities selectively, in light of everything else your organization has to accomplish.

14. *Develop Subcultural Plan*

Once you have set priorities within the subcultures, engage as many associates as possible in the cultural renewal planning process. The subcultural priorities will help identify the initiatives to be assigned to specific leaders and associates within each of the subcultures. The goals and objectives outlined in earlier chapters will aid in identifying these specific initiatives within the particular subcultures.

The goal is to develop initiatives in the subcultures that carry their own measurable goals and objectives and that complement the overarching objectives, goals, strategies and tactics of the larger enterprise. The result should be the creation of vital cultural processes that complement and enhance the entire organization's operating processes.

15. *Execute Subcultural Plan*

When priorities are established and assignments agreed upon, the next step is to launch the cultural renewal process. This entails making sure associates throughout the subculture are clear on what the current initiatives are, how they are personally involved and how they will be affected. By monitoring results at least every quarter, continuously coaching associates and providing timely feedback, you will better be able to keep the process on course, and to make any necessary adjustments.

16. *Evaluate Cultural Changes*

As the year progresses, personally evaluate and document changes occurring in the cultural landscape of your organization. Discussing these changes with other leaders and associates will provide valuable feedback that allows you to intensify positive efforts and to maximize the return on the most important initiatives.

As the year draws to a close, evaluate the progress made and begin to develop a new set of priorities for the coming year. The end of the year is also a good time to conduct another survey, either formally or informally, to gain insight into associates' perceptions about the first year of cultural renewal as a basis for creating priorities or making adjustments for the following year.

Don't forget to celebrate your cultural successes. Drawing positive attention to examples of cultural gains will inspire deeper commitment and broader participation in individual and group efforts to improve the organization's culture.

17. *Annual Cycle*

Now that your organization has committed to the renewal process, it is crucial as part of the annual planning process that cultural leaders reassess the strengths of the organization, using the six cultural elements as guides.

This is also the time to validate the priorities required to take the culture to the next level of organizational effectiveness. These priorities should result in specific initiatives that inform the actions of leaders and associates in standard business planning and in setting goals for the year. By getting into the habit of continuously monitoring and reacting to the cultural needs of the organization, leaders hone their cultural skills and make decisions that are guided by the core values that define the organization. They become strong cultural models that inspire associates to mirror their behavior.

The journey that might at first have seemed arduous and overwhelming now begins to feel more natural and energizing. Committed leadership will inspire stamina for improved operating results, satisfied associates and an agile organization that can adapt quickly to the new demands of the marketplace and the changing needs of its customers.

Think of your initial steps on this journey as a process of renewing and revitalizing your skills and abilities as a leader, one who will be able to provide stronger direction and motivation than

Cultural renewal is a never-ending journey

ever before. You might also think of your efforts to become a strong cultural leader as a gift to the organization, and to each individual associate as well.

Bon voyage! I know you'll have a great and profitable journey.

CHAPTER 10

Making the Case for Change

"By far the biggest mistake people make when trying to change organizations is to plunge ahead without establishing a high enough sense of urgency in fellow managers and employees."

—John P. Kotter
Author, *Leading Change* [35]

This brief chapter summarizes key points that underscore the power of cultural leadership to assist you in anticipating and answering questions and challenges from others in your organization as you set out on your journey of cultural renewal. These points are offered in a question-and-answer format to help you get started immediately on your quest for a more effective workplace culture.

You are the catalyst for making a case for change

What is organizational culture?

Culture is the glue that holds together the values, beliefs, attitudes and expectations of an organization. It reflects the formal and informal processes being carried out in getting things done. Culture might be summed up as "the way we do things around here."

Why should we attempt to build a more effective culture?

1. To improve the operating results of our organization
2. To improve the ability of our organization to attract, motivate and retain top talent
3. To ensure that our organization appropriately adapts to changing conditions

Can organizations have more than one culture?

Yes. Often we think of the enterprise as a single workplace culture. But, in reality, there are many cultures within an enterprise. Every division and department should be seen as a subculture of its overarching culture. In addition to formal organizational cultures, informal cultures are represented by the casual acquaintanceships that emerge in the lunchroom or the deeper friendships that form between officemates.

The lasting performance of an enterprise often depends on whether its subcultures also are strong, adaptive cultures that support the overarching culture.

Who is responsible for creating cultural leadership and what must they know?

Ideally, cultural leadership starts with the CEO, but not necessarily. Leaders can create great organizational cultures at every level of their organizations.

Whether you are leading a giant corporation or a small work team, you have the ability, and the responsibility, to strive for an improved workplace culture.

Every leader of a viable enterprise has more than enough freedom and resources to dramatically improve the workplace culture. For this reason, leaders at all levels need to understand and assume their responsibility for cultural leadership.

Why is it important to gain full commitment to cultural change?

Cultural leaders must be committed and motivated themselves in order to motivate and inspire their associates. It is also very important to effectively engage and excite all of the associates within the organization concerning the cultural renewal process and their role in it.

Subcultural leaders must be able to provide objective, and often difficult, assessments of the strengths and weaknesses of their respective subcultures within the context of the overarching culture.

How does the Visionomics Cube mirror organizational culture?

The Visionomics model is made up of the critical elements of culture—core values, products and services, direction, structure, measurements and rewards—that must be developed both individually and in relation to each other to maximize the potential of the organization. In many cases the elements are completely missing or are latent in terms of their effect on the organization. Culture is like a puzzle that can be solved by bringing all the appropriate pieces together.

Isn't this just another management "flavor of the month"?

Almost any initiative that is begun without commitment will fail. As cultural leaders, we have a responsibility to continuously improve our culture to make our organization as effective as possible.

Unlike some other management programs the Visionomics model allows us to accurately assess the present state of our culture and then develop and implement a plan of cultural renewal based on the priorities of our organization.

What further makes this model unique is that it provides a process of continuous cultural renewal that involves everyone in the organization, rather than reflecting a top-down, hierarchical approach to change.

For these reasons, the Visionomics model provides the framework or context for cultural renewal and a pathway for leaders to follow in improving cultural performance.

But won't these organizational changes consume a lot of valuable time and resources?

The Visionomics model offers an opportunity to improve the effectiveness of our culture from the moment we first embrace this journey of renewal. Time invested on specific cultural renewal initiatives will be returned many times over through improvements in overall organizational effectiveness. Can we afford not to improve our organization's effectiveness?

Although our resources may not be optimum, we can work with the resources we have now to begin the process, which will result in greater resources as our productivity improves.

Why bother defining our core values?

Every organization has values of one kind or another. The question is whether to leave them to chance or choose values that complement and support the goals and objectives of the organization.

Positive core values lay the foundation for a high-performance workplace culture. Until we decide what those values will be, and how we will interact with each other, it's difficult to be the best we can be at anything else.

We already have our mission statement and values posted on every wall. Isn't that enough?

For values to be truly effective, they must be an integral part of the organization. Cultural leaders and every associate must communicate these values daily through their words and actions, or the values become meaningless phrases.

Identifying core values and modeling them for associates is the first step in this process of continuous cultural renewal that will benefit everyone.

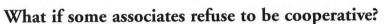

What if some associates refuse to be cooperative?

Values are critical to the organization's success. To instill values successfully, they must be enforced and reinforced. If you don't do that, then the lowest standard of values you are willing to tolerate becomes your true core values, not what you post on the wall.

If an associate can't or won't live up to the values chosen by the organization, you must hold him or her accountable, so that other associates can feel confident that you are serious about your commitment.

Where do we begin?

If you are starting the process of cultural renewal from scratch, the priorities are to:

- Identify core values
- Determine the level of customer satisfaction and need for change
- Establish each of the directional components (purpose, vision, strategy, tactics and goals)
- Develop a plan for a ensuring organizational capacity and process effectiveness
- Define objective measurements and commit to them
- Develop a system for effective compensation and recognition

As the process is refined, you will develop a routine that:

- Uses objective assessments to establish priorities for change
- Sets specific and measurable goals and objectives for improvement
- Initiates action and seeks stakeholder feedback
- Tracks and measures results
- Regularly reports progress
- Celebrates successes and recognizes associates who made it possible

What are the key questions a leader should ask in assessing where and how to begin?

- Do I have the knowledge and commitment to begin the cultural renewal process?
- Do our associates want a better culture?

- Can we create enthusiasm and commitment for cultural change within our organization?
- Do we have a compelling vision of what we want our culture to look like?
- Does everyone believe we can get there?
- Do all of our stakeholders understand their roles in this cultural renewal process?

When and how shall we celebrate our success?

Cultural renewal is a journey full of new challenges, exciting discoveries and measurable successes. You can develop an enriching culture that can adapt to changing conditions, attract and motivate talented associates, increase productivity and dramatically improve the bottom line.

In the process, you will create an invigorating and rewarding environment that you and your associates will want to celebrate based on the large as well as the small successes you experience individually and collectively along the way.

How you celebrate your successes is up to you and your team, but they will surely come. Begin now to plan for them.

Endnotes

1. Eisen, Lewis D., & Siegel, Jonathan P., *The Manager's Book of Quotations* (New York: Amacom, 1991), p. 351.

2. Denison, Daniel, *Corporate Culture and Organizational Effectiveness* (Ann Arbor, MI: Aviat, 1997).

3. Schein, Edgar H., *Organizational Culture and Leadership* - second edition (San Francisco: Jossey-Bass Publishers, 1992), p. 374.

4. Denison, *Corporate Culture and Organizational Effectiveness*, p. 2.

5. Stein, Nicholas, "The World's Most Admired Companies: Measuring People Power," *Fortune*, Vol. 142, No. 7, October 2, 2000, pp. 182-196.

6. Former General Electric CEO Jack Welch's address to shareowners at the annual shareowners' meeting in Richmond, Virginia, April 26, 2000.

7. Personal communication, September 2000.

8. Blanchard, Kenneth, & O'Connor, Michael, *Managing by Values* (San Francisco: Berrett-Koehler Publications, 1997), p. 73.

9. Flynn, Gillian, "It Takes Values to Capitalize on Change," *Workforce*, Vol. 76, April 1997, pp. 27-32.

10. The values determination process was co-developed by Joe Fisher and Dutch Landen in 1992. Joe uses it in his consulting work for team building. The original list includes 44 words and definitions to determine a group's important values. I have added to the list now over 50 words and definitions.

11. Meyer, Christopher, *Fast Cycle Time* (New York: Macmillan, Inc., 1993), p. 7.

12. Case, John, "Corporate Culture," *Inc.*, Vol. 18, No. 16, November 1996, pp. 42-49.

13. ibid., p. 42.

14. Fisher, Anne, "The 100 Best Companies to Work for in America," *Fortune*, Vol. 137, No. 1, January 12, 1998, pp. 68-70.

15. Finegan, Jay, "Everything According to Plan," *Inc.*, March 1995, pp. 78-85.

16. Covey, Stephen R., Merrill, A. Roger, & Merrill, Rebecca R., *First Things First* (New York: Simon & Schuster, 1994), pp. 103-104.

17. George W. Merck, speech at the Medical College of Virginia at Richmond, December 1, 1950, courtesy Merck & Company historical archives. Quote taken from Collins, James C., & Porras, Jerry I., *Built to Last* (New York: Harperbusiness, 1994), p. 48.

18. Collins, James C., & Porras, Jerry I., *Built to Last* (New York: Harperbusiness, 1994), pp. 76-77.

19. ibid., p. 56. Original source: David Packard, "A Management Code of Ethics," speech presented to the American Management Association, San Francisco, January 24, 1958, courtesy Hewlett-Packard Company archives.

20. Bartlett, John, & Kaplan, Justin, editors, *Familiar Quotations* (Boston: Little, Brown & Co., 1992), p. 741.

21. Barker, Joel A., "The Power of Vision" (video) (Burnsville, MN: ChartHouse International Learning Corporation, 1991).

22. Fred Lyons, president of Marion Laboratories. (Fred was president of Marion and MMD until he was named chairman of MMD in 1992 and retired as chairman of HMR in 1995.) Speech at Marion Leadership Conference in winter of 1982.

23. As quoted in Freiberg, Kevin, & Freiberg, Jackie, *Nuts!* (New York: Broadway Books, 1996), p. 77.

24. Peg Neuhauser, co-author of *Culture.Com* interview with Linda Rutherford, senior manager for public relations at Southwest Airlines, June 4, 2000. www.culturedotcom.com/article_3.htm, "Southwest Airlines: On How to Build a Culture With Speed As One of The Key Characteristics."

25. Sherman, Stratford, "Secrets of HP's 'Muddled' Team," *Fortune*, Vol. 133, No. 5, March 18, 1996, pp. 116-119.

26. First introduced by Michie Slaughter, VP of Human Resources, Marion Laboratories, Kansas City, MO, at an internal training and development program in 1983. The balanced decision-making process helped associates consider the interests of the stakeholder(s) most impacted by the decision.

27. Kaydos, Will, *Measuring, Managing, and Maximizing Performance* (Portland, OR: Productivity Press, 1991), p. 51.

28. Nelson, Bob, *1001 Ways to Reward Employees* (New York: Workman Publishing Co., 1994), p. xv.

29. Maslow, Abraham H., "A Theory of Human Motivation," *Psychological Review*, 1943, 50, pp. 370-396.

30. McCoy, Thomas, *Compensation and Motivation: Maximizing Employee Performance with Behavior-Based Incentive Plans* (New York: Amacom, 1992).

31. Fisher, "The 100 Best Companies to Work for in America," pp. 68-70.

32. Grant, Linda, "Happy Workers, High Returns," *Fortune*, Vol. 137, No. 1, January 12, 1998, p. 81.

33. Schein, Edgar H., *The Corporate Culture Survival Guide* (San Francisco: Jossey-Bass Publishers, 1999), p. 185.

34. The Visionomics Cultural Conscience is a software program developed by Dave Raden and Jerry Haney with outside programming support. It is intended to enable leaders to evaluate the strengths and weaknesses of each cultural element in their organization and plan for cultural improvement. To order, contact Visionomics, Inc., 107 Shoreview Court, Lee's Summit, MO 64064, 816-373-3074, E:mail: info@visionomics.com.

35. Kotter, John P., *Leading Change* (Boston: Harvard Business School Press, 1996), p. 4.

Bibliography

Austin, Robert D., *Measuring and Managing Performance in Organizations.* New York: Dorset House Publishing Co., 1996.

Barker, Joel A., "The Power of Vision" (video). Burnsville, MN: ChartHouse International Learning Corporation, 1991.

Barker Joel A., *Paradigms: The Business of Discovering the Future.* New York: HarperBusiness, 1993.

Bartlett, John, & Kaplan, Justin, editors, *Familiar Quotations.* Boston: Little, Brown & Co., 1992.

Blanchard, Kenneth, & O'Connor, Michael, *Managing by Values.* San Francisco: Berrett-Koehler Publications, 1997.

Case, John, "Corporate Culture," *Inc.*, Vol. 18, No. 16, November 1996, pp. 42-49.

Collins, James C., & Porras , Jerry I., *Built to Last: Successful Habits of Visionary Companies.* New York: Harpercollins, 1994.

Covey, Stephen R., Merrill, A. Roger, & Merrill, Rebecca R., *First Things First.* New York: Simon & Schuster, 1994.

Denison, Daniel, *Corporate Culture and Organizational Effectiveness.* Ann Arbor, MI: Aviat, 1997.

Denison, Daniel R., & Neale, William S., *Denison Organizational Culture Survey.* Ann Arbor, MI: Aviat, 1998.

Eisen, Lewis D., & Siegel, Jonathan P., *The Manager's Book of Quotations.* New York: Amacom, 1991.

Finegan, Jay, "Everything According to Plan," *Inc.*, March 1995, pp. 78-85.

Fisher, Anne, "The 100 Best Companies to Work for in America," *Fortune*, Vol. 137, No. 1, January 12, 1998, pp. 68-70.

Flynn, Gillian, "It Takes Values to Capitalize on Change," *Workforce*, Vol. 76, April 1997, pp. 27-32.

Freiberg, Kevin, & Freiberg, Jackie, *Nuts!* New York: Broadway Books, 1996.

Grant, Linda, "Happy Workers, High Returns," *Fortune*, Vol. 137, No. 1, January 12, 1998, p. 81.

Kaydos, Will, *Measuring, Managing, and Maximizing Performance.* Portland, OR: Productivity Press, 1994.

Kotter, John P., *Leading Change.* Boston: Harvard Business School Press, 1996.

Kotter, John P., & Heskett, James L., *Corporate Culture and Performance.* New York: Free Press, 1992.

Maslow, Abraham H., "A Theory of Human Motivation," *Psychological Review*, 1943, 50, pp. 370-396.

McCoy, Thomas J., *Compensation and Motivation, Maximizing Employee Preformance with Behavior-Based Incentive Plans*. New York: Amacom, 1992.

Meyer, Christopher, *Fast Cycle Time*. New York: Macmillan, Inc., 1993.

Nelson, Bob, *1001 Ways to Reward Employees*. New York: Workman Publishing Co., 1994.

Schein, Edgar H., *Organizational Culture and Leadership* - second edition. San Francisco: Jossey-Bass Publishers, 1992.

Schein, Edgar H., *The Corporate Culture Survival Guide*. San Francisco: Jossey-Bass Publishers, 1999.

Sherman, Stratford, "Secrets of HP's 'Muddled' Team," *Fortune*, Vol. 133, No. 5, March 18, 1996, pp. 116-119.

Stein, Nicholas, "The World's Most Admired Companies: Measuring People Power," *Fortune*, Vol. 142, No. 7, October 2, 2000, pp. 182-196.

Websites

Eriksen, Greg, "Why They Threw the Books Open at Springfield Remanufacturing Corp.," Foundation for Enterprise Development, *http://www.fed.org*

National Performance Review, White House Office of Management and Budget "Primer on Performance Measurement," revised 1995, *http://govinfo.library.unt.edu/npr/library/resource/gpraprmr.html*

O'Brien, William J., "Character and the Corporation," a series of essays, *http://www..solonline.org/res/wp/15001.html*

About SRC, Springfield Remanufacturing Corp., *http://srcreman.com/src-main.html*

Stewart, Douglas, *Management and Training, Growing the Corporate Culture*, First Union, *http://www.firstunion.com/smallbusiness/rescenter/hr/research_corp_cult.html*

Welch, John F., Jr., *speeches*, General Electric, *http://www.ge.com/news/welch/speeches/roads.htm*

"Southwest Airlines: On How to Build a Culture With Speed As One of The Key Characteristics," at *www.culturedotcom.com/article_3.htm*

Index

(Photocopy this order form)

MAKING CULTURE PAY

SOLVING THE PUZZLE *of* ORGANIZATIONAL EFFECTIVENESS

JERRY HANEY

Price per copy: $29.95

Name

Company

Address

City/State/Zip

Phone Number

E-mail

Mastercard/Visa

_____ – _____ – _____ – _____   Quantity ordered

Expiration date _____/_____   Subtotal

Signature   Sales tax*

Shipping and handling**

Total

Please make checks payable to Visionomics, Inc.
Quantity orders invited. Write for bulk account
prices.

*Please add Missouri sales tax
of 6.6% for books shipped to
MIssouri addresses.

**Please add $4 shipping and
handling for first book, $1.50
for additional books.

Send to:
Visionomics, Inc.
107 Shoreview Court
Lee's Summit, MO 64064

Phone/fax: 816-373-3074
or visit our website: www.visionomics.com

Please send information about
Jerry Haney's presentation
Making Culture Pay.

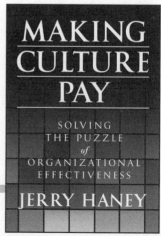